Suzy Wengel

The Scandi Sense Diet

Lose weight and keep it off with the life-changing handful method

MITCHELL BEAZLEY

Table of contents

Common sense helped me lose 88 pounds

I can still remember the sight of my gigantic thighs next to the tiny newborn body of my youngest son. I weighed almost 220lb (100kg) and it wasn't just pregnancy weight. As a small woman of around 5ft 3in (163cm) tall, 220lb (100kg) is a lot. I felt less attractive and energetic than ever, and I had been feeling this way for a while.

I snored. I often had a cold. I had heart palpitations and constantly felt listless and tired. My allergies were out of control and I was taking large doses of medicine to keep them in check. On a warm day, I sweated so much that I had to wear inserts under my armpits so I wasn't dripping with sweat. My breasts were huge and my stomach was hanging so much that I had a fungal infection growing underneath. I found myself in the category doctors call 'Obesity Class II'.

Fortunately, that day in the maternity ward in April 2011 was a turning point for me. During my pregnancy, I had promised myself that I would get down to a healthy weight and leave behind all the bad habits that had made me fat. I just had to give birth first.

As I lay there in bed with an oxygen tube up my nose, connected to a drip with my newborn baby in my arms, I felt the strength well up inside me to make the decision: I wanted to be a strong, stable weight and a healthy mother for my children.

When I think back to that time, I see a picture of myself sitting in a huge bell jar of fat. That image is associated with many emotions: claustrophobia, desperation and loneliness, but also a strange sort of security. Security, because it is much easier to stick to familiar habits than to form new ones. Little by little, I had defined myself as a chubby girl and I had accepted that I would never be any different. I couldn't even consider the idea of leaving my comfort zone – because what would be on the other side? How much deprivation would be

"

As I lay there in bed with an oxygen tube up my nose, connected to a drip with my newborn baby in my arms, I felt the strength well up inside me to make the decision: I wanted to be a strong, stable weight and a healthy mother for my children.

necessary to just stay slim? In order to break that pattern, I had to confront myself with this question: How could I have let my weight escalate so far without stopping myself? I still don't have a simple answer.

I can clearly remember when my weight problems began, however. It was when I changed school in year seven. At my old school, I had been bullied and had never felt like part of the community. When I moved schools, everything changed. I finally made some friends and found my place in the flock. At the same time, I became very aware of how my body, and my friends' bodies, looked. I compared myself to the other girls who, in my eyes, looked slim and lovely. I wanted to look like them – tiny, with thin legs. I could see that was how the popular girls looked.

When I started secondary school, which is at the age of 15 in Denmark, I weighed about 146lb (66kg). I wasn't overweight – just healthy and shapely.

However, I couldn't see that myself. When I looked in the mirror, I saw a girl with short, fat legs and crooked teeth. I didn't want to look like that. There began my 18-year fight with my weight, a battle that, as the years went by, became increasingly strenuous and wearing as I put on more and more weight.

One day I called my doctor in desperation and told him about my situation – namely, that I needed his help because all my own attempts to lose weight had ended in failure. The consultation lasted no more than five minutes and at the end of the call, he wrote me a prescription for diet pills. The pills worked as intended and I lost weight, but as soon as I stopped taking them, the pounds piled on to my body once more.

I continued in this way for years. I followed all the current slimming trends, testing out one diet after another. At times I lived exclusively on pasta and cheese or rice pudding

99

In my wardrobe, there were clothes ranging from size 10 to 18. I used to buy the same item of clothing in several sizes, so that I could wear it no matter where I was on my weight curve.

with cinnamon sugar, and at other times I completely starved myself.

I repeatedly lost 44–66lb (20–30kg) and put it back on again, gaining a little more weight each time. The pounds crept up on me insidiously over the years and I adapted my life just as gradually to a body that was constantly changing in size.

In my wardrobe, there were clothes ranging from size 10 to 18. I used to buy the same item of clothing in several sizes, so that I could wear it no matter where I was on my weight curve.

At that time, I was quite physically active, so the reason for the extra pounds wasn't that I was spending my days lying on the sofa eating. My weight gain was almost certainly because I was eating the wrong food. I loved calorie-packed meals: white bread with honey, chocolate spread or cheese; cornflakes with lots of sugar; pasta; pizza and burgers.

In my early twenties, my eating habits changed so often that my weight was constantly fluctuating. At times, I was only a few pounds overweight, at others – when I wasn't on a diet – I was decidedly overweight.

Looking back, I can see that I was overeating. I lived in a blinkered, black and white world. Either I threw myself, frothing at the mouth, at everything I felt like eating, without questioning it, or everything was completely off limits because I was on a diet. Whenever a diet fell flat – and it always did at some point – I felt like a huge failure, and then I let loose again on the overeating. In those moments, nothing really mattered.

The change in my eating habits came about after a particularly bad break-up with a boyfriend. From one day to the next, I was suddenly living alone. It was a big upheaval; I felt lonely and at the same time I was struggling with a lovesickness that I tried to relieve with food. And it

I would wolf down half a loaf of white bread with chocolate spread while Jesper was out of the house for a short while. Similarly, I would skilfully and swiftly conceal packaging that would reveal that I had just consumed four or five ice lollies.

was easy – there was no-one to see what I was eating, so I could let go of control completely.

I kept my misery and my overeating to myself. I had become an expert at putting up a façade when I was with other people – I was always the happy, smiling one. No one had any idea that deep inside I was an unhappy person fighting a bitter battle. I was deeply dissatisfied with myself and my appearance, and I quickly became surly and sad. I wanted to dig myself into a hole and indulge my destructive thoughts, because how on earth could I improve my situation?

In 2005, Jesper and I fell for each other and we soon moved in together. At that time, I weighed about 190lb (86kg) and was trapped in a pattern that fluctuated between overeating and restrictive dieting.

Thoughts on my weight and the food I was eating or not eating occupied far too many of my waking hours.

I developed strategies for eating surreptitiously and subsequently covering my tracks.

I would wolf down half a loaf of white bread with chocolate spread while Jesper was out of the house for a short while. Similarly, I would skilfully and swiftly hide packaging that would reveal that I had just consumed four or five ice lollies.

I would also buy two bags of toffees and transfer the contents from one bag into the other, so it looked like I had only bought a single bag. Overeating was a secret of which I was deeply ashamed.

In hindsight, it is a little scary that these deception tactics were such a big part of my life, even though I was head over heels in love. This new chapter of my life made me want to pull myself together and lose weight for good. I was fed up of never being happy with myself. Every time we went into town, I left with a feeling

of depression because I didn't look good, no matter how many hours I had spent in front of the mirror. I felt that my legs were still too heavy and that my eyelids were enveloped in fat.

I thought it was embarrassing that I couldn't just pull myself together and control my weight. I would concoct reasons to cancel a social engagement – just to avoid being looked at.

I was constantly thinking about losing weight; I felt like I was on a never-ending diet. Even so, my weight never changed significantly. I was trapped in an unhealthy pattern of hunger and overeating that cancelled each other out.

But then something happened – on Christmas Eve 2007, Jesper proposed to me and I said yes. At that time, I had an exact picture of how I wanted to look at our wedding and it wasn't the size 18 that I was at that moment. I had five months to lose weight before the wedding. I managed to reach my goal through intense effort – I walked or jogged to and from work every day and was very consistent with my diet.

We were married on 17 May 2008. My wedding dress was a size 10. It was wonderful to be standing there with my slim hourglass waist in my dream wedding dress. But neither the joy nor the dress size lasted, because I couldn't, of course, maintain the strict regime I had set for myself.

I began overeating again the day after the wedding – to an intense degree. I thought that, as I had reached my goal, I could let go. It was as if I was desperately trying to catch up with all those calories that both my body and my mind had missed over the past five months.

"

The doctor asked me why I didn't have control of my diet and my body, when I seemed to have control of my life in all other areas. The question really hit home.

I put on almost 44lb (20kg) in no time. Then I became pregnant, and after the birth of our first son, Valdemar, in 2010, my weight had risen to almost 200lb (90kg). One day, I went to my doctor with Valdemar for a check-up and I was confronted on my eating habits for the first time. The doctor asked me why I didn't have control of my diet and my body, when I seemed to have control of my life in all other areas. The question really hit home. Two months later, however, I became pregnant once more so I let go of the reins and ate freely – without restraint.

My doctor's question had planted a seed, however. It was that question that made me decide that I would take serious steps with my obesity once I had given birth to our second child, Albert; not a day, a week or a month after I had given birth, but the moment he came into the world. And when that moment came, I had no doubt at all.

I decided to tackle the weight loss completely differently this time.

No quick fix, no starvation diet, no heavy exercise, which I wouldn't be able to keep up anyway. No, this time I would use my common sense and find a way that suited me.

I had to lower my expectations and recognize that things aren't always black and white. And I realized that I needed a fixed structure to reach my goal of a lasting change in my lifestyle. So I spent a great deal of my second pregnancy reading about nutrition and familiarizing myself with diet research. I came to understand that it was good to have protein, vegetables and fat if you want to live healthily and lose weight. And I learned that a varied diet and lasting change in lifestyle make a difference. With that knowledge under my belt, I started from scratch.

For long periods of my life, I was unable to recognize when I was full. That is why I ate constantly, regardless of what signals my brain was sending to me. Now my system works as it

99

For long periods of my life, I was unable to recognize when I was full. That is why I ate constantly, regardless of what signals my brain was sending to me. Now my system works as it should, but it took three years for my body to learn to tune into the natural signals of feeling full.

should, but it took three years for my body to learn to tune into the natural signals of feeling full.

In the beginning, I had to test out my ideas to make progress, so it was particularly important for me to have structure and direction. I quickly realized that if I always ate so that I was full, three meals a day pretty much suited me.

At the same time, three daily meals gave me a structure that I could stick to. If I felt hungry an hour after I had eaten, I would understand that it wasn't real hunger, so I drank a glass of water instead of eating.

It worked! In nine months I lost 88lb (40kg) and I've kept to that weight ever since. At the same time, my energy levels increased significantly with my weight loss. I had more energy to play with my children because I didn't get out of breath from the smallest bit of activity.

Suddenly, I didn't need an afternoon nap on the sofa either. The weight loss affected my whole life. My mood improved, my energy reserves grew, my skin became better and I got my allergies under control.

In addition, I gained the space and energy to think about a whole lot more than food and weight. I don't think it would be an exaggeration to say that, before the weight loss, my head was 90 per cent filled up with negative thoughts and speculation about my weight. After the weight loss, there was nothing more to worry about in that respect so it was a huge release. I love the physical and mental calm that has followed my escape from overeating hell. It is tricky to put into words, but I've been released from my bell jar and am back in reality – a reality worth living in.

After cracking the code for weight loss, I wanted to share my method with other people. Just think, what if I could help other overweight people

to find a similar freedom? I qualified as a dietitian, and at the same time I set myself the task of writing down everything that I had learnt during my journey. I knew that I wanted my method to rely on common sense and simplicity. I wanted to help people to escape the monotony of calorie counting and weighing food. Last but not least, I wanted to get away from a restrictive eating model where things are either healthy or unhealthy.

That's why I constructed the idea of the handful principle and meal-boxes – that is, the system you can read about in this book. Today I eat everything with great enjoyment and without any guilt. I hope you get as much enjoyment out of the Scandi Sense diet as I have.

Suzy Wengel

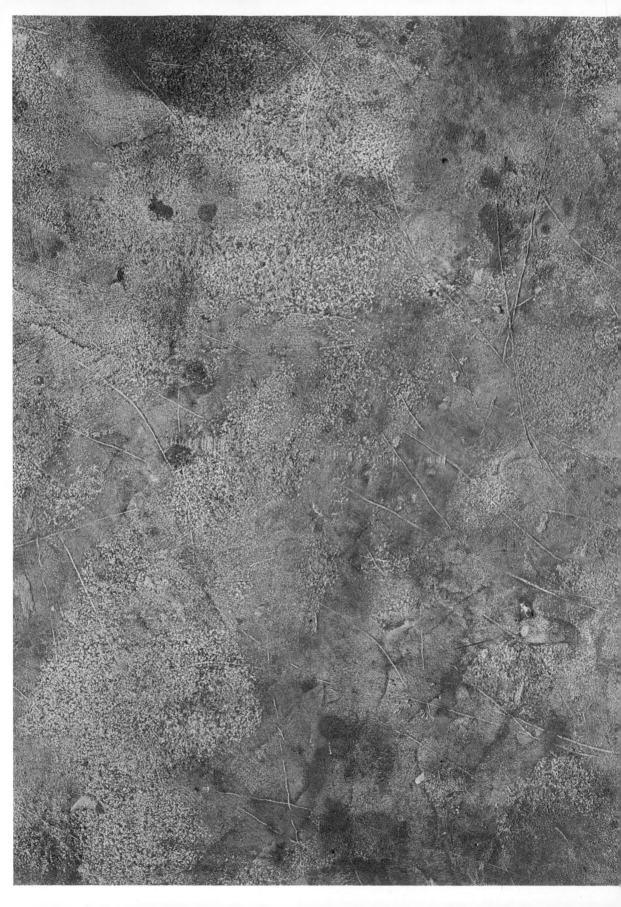

What
Scandi Sense
is all about

The name Scandi Sense is inspired by the notion of 'common sense'. It is no coincidence that I have chosen this particular name; as well as being simple and straightforward, Scandi Sense is based on common sense in relation to the composition and amount of food we choose to eat.

Scandi Sense is intended to be suitable for everyone, regardless of size and weight, and is therefore more a lifestyle than a diet. The basic idea is that you eat a Scandi Sense version of the food you usually have. This means that you won't have to overhaul your diet entirely – it will just need adjusting. This makes it more likely that the lifestyle will last in the long run.

For example, if you make spaghetti bolognese for the whole family, you will eat less spaghetti and more bolognese sauce than you might have previously. At the same time, you'll put a lot of vegetables into the bolognese

sauce and possibly supplement it with a green salad. You can also add some extra flavour by sprinkling cheese on top, because in Scandi Sense, you don't have to be afraid of fat. In moderation, fat is good for the body and, of course, it often adds extra flavour to your food.

Scandi Sense isn't a ready-made diet plan, but some simple principles to live by – principles that will give you the right balance of nutrients and ensure that you maintain a stable blood sugar level throughout the day. The Scandi Sense diet is based on the official dietary advice of the Danish Health Board. The basic idea is that if you fill yourself up with balanced, healthy meals, you won't be so easily tempted by food that will make you gain weight. You also get a mental tool, namely the 'meal-boxes', to help you fit yummy things such as a piece of cake into your diet.

Whilst nothing is forbidden by Scandi Sense, there are some foods that you

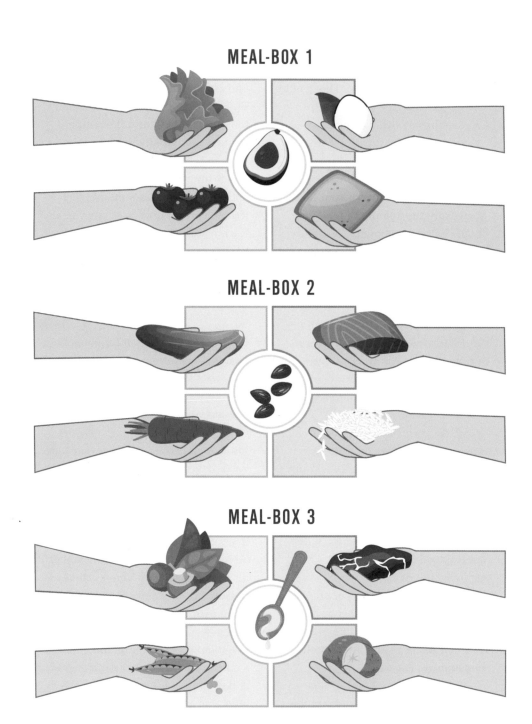

MEAL-BOX 1

MEAL-BOX 2

MEAL-BOX 3

READ MORE ABOUT WHAT YOUR HANDFULS SHOULD CONTAIN ON PAGE 22.

should enjoy in limited quantities, or compensate for at other meals. I call these foods 'indulgences'. They could be sweets, cake, ice cream, crisps, tortilla chips or sweet drinks.

HANDFULS AND MEAL-BOXES

You will use the palms of your hands to measure the amount of food you should eat at each meal. You can eat up to four handfuls of food for each meal, and if they are properly balanced you will easily feel full.

Because the size of our hands is most often related to our build and our height, this will work out as on average 1,500 calories a day for women and for men a little more, around 2,000 calories a day.

If food is prepared according to the Scandi Sense principles, the amounts will enable you to lose on average 0.9–1.8lb (400–800g) at a measured pace per week until the goal weight is achieved. Your goal weight is the weight that suits the lifestyle you are happy with.

As men generally require a little more food than women, I have included recipes suitable for both men and women.

If cooking for both men and women in your household, you can double up the woman's portion and just check how much extra protein, starch/fruit and fat the man's portion requires. The amount of vegetables is usually the same for both and the recipe method is generally the same.

The Scandi Sense meal-boxes are both a practical and a mental tool to help you keep track of your meals. Each meal-box represents a meal. You should imagine that you have three meal-boxes a day available, each filled with your four handfuls of food plus 1–3 tablespoons of fat.

If there is sometimes a little extra food in a meal-box, or maybe food that wasn't planned, just close that meal-box and carry on, without beating yourself up or feeling guilty.

Think about people who have always had a healthy weight. They also eat too much food, or too many calories, on occasion, and they do so without reproaching themselves. You have to get away from thinking, 'Now it's all ruined, so it doesn't really matter', because it is exactly that reaction that causes the failure of so many attempts to eat healthily.

If you have strayed from the plan at a meal, rather than stressing over it, it is a much better strategy to be proactive and get straight back into a good rhythm with the next meal-box.

THREE MEALS A DAY

There is no evidence to suggest that it is better to eat six times a day rather than three. Some people thrive on more meals daily, while others are fine with fewer.

But there is no doubt that the risk of eating too many calories is greater when you eat more times a day.

With three daily meals, it is easier to keep blood sugar levels stable, especially when meals are sensibly planned using the Sense Meal-Box Model (see pages 34–35). Following this model, the metabolism doesn't drop significantly when you cut down on the number of meals. It is healthy for the body to have a break between meals, not only for blood sugar levels, but also for your mental wellbeing and your intestinal system.

Finally, it is good to allow yourself to feel hungry sometimes! It helps you to achieve a natural regulation of how much you eat.

When your meal-boxes are filled with nourishing, filling food, you won't crave yummy things to the same extent as you might do with lots of daily meals of different sizes.

I recommend that you follow the Sense Meal-Box Model strictly for the first 14 days.

Fill out a diet plan so that you are sure you are getting the right amount of food. You can find a template on page 67, which you can photocopy and fill in.

You will probably find that you don't need snacks in between meals and that there is a certain freedom in only eating three times a day.

After the first two weeks you will be in a position to determine how many meals you need and tailor your eating pattern accordingly.

HUNGER BAROMETER

If, after the first 14 days of Scandi Sense, you still struggle to work out when you are hungry and when you are full, just continue to follow the Scandi Sense principles strictly.

Once you feel ready to stand on your own two feet, it is time to familiarize yourself with the hunger barometer.

Think of your appetite as something that can be measured on a hunger barometer, from zero to ten. Zero is 'not hungry at all' and ten is 'totally famished'. The idea is that you are ready to have a meal according to the Sense Meal-Box Model (see pages 34–35) when you land on around 7 or 8 on the hunger barometer.

It also means that it is okay to eat a late breakfast if you aren't hungry the moment you get up. Or have a late dinner, if it fits better with your lifestyle. It is a myth that breakfast is the most important meal of the day and it is also a myth that everything you eat after 6pm will make you put on weight!

Once you have become familiar with your own hunger signals and only eat when you are hungry, you will eventually, using the Sense Meal-Box Model, know how much food you need to sustain you for 5–6 hours, and will find yourself naturally wanting a meal when you land on 7 or 8 on your hunger barometer. Once you have eaten, you will be back down to 0 on the barometer – and after 5–6 hours you will return to 7 or 8. In this way you will find an eating pattern that suits you. The eating pattern isn't set in stone – it may vary from day to day and from season to season.

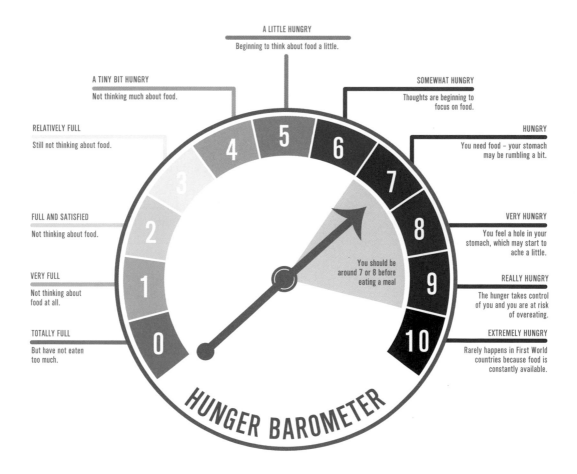

A LITTLE HUNGRY
Beginning to think about food a little.

A TINY BIT HUNGRY
Not thinking much about food.

SOMEWHAT HUNGRY
Thoughts are beginning to focus on food.

RELATIVELY FULL
Still not thinking about food.

HUNGRY
You need food – your stomach may be rumbling a bit.

FULL AND SATISFIED
Not thinking about food.

VERY HUNGRY
You feel a hole in your stomach, which may start to ache a little.

VERY FULL
Not thinking about food at all.

You should be around 7 or 8 before eating a meal

REALLY HUNGRY
The hunger takes control of you and you are at risk of overeating.

TOTALLY FULL
But have not eaten too much.

EXTREMELY HUNGRY
Rarely happens in First World countries because food is constantly available.

HUNGER BAROMETER

Scandi Sense

HANDFUL
1 (+2)

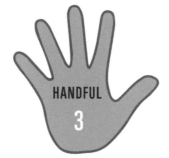

HANDFUL
3

HANDFUL
4

 VEGETABLES

c.100–250g

1–2 handfuls

 PROTEIN

c.100–200g

MEAT
POULTRY
FISH
LOW-FAT CHEESE
(max. 17% fat)

1 handful = 2–3 eggs

 STARCH AND /OR FRUIT

BREAD
PASTA
RICE
POTATOES
MUESLI (less than 13g of sugar per 100g)
FRUIT/BERRIES

Choose wholemeal
1 HANDFUL =
100ml oatmeal,
1 piece of fruit
or 1 slice of bread

N.B. This handful can be replaced by up to ½ Handful 3 (protein) and possibly more vegetables.

 1–3 TABLESPOONS OF FAT PER MEAL

8–10g of 'pure fat' per tablespoon

COCONUT OIL
OLIVE OIL
BUTTER
MAYONNAISE
NUTS/KERNELS
PESTO
DARK CHOCOLATE
(min. 70% cocoa solids)
CHEESE (18% fat or above)
3 TABLESPOONS = ½ a large avocado

REMEMBER: 3 MEALS A DAY – ONLY WHEN HUNGRY

At least 2 of your 3 daily meals shall contain this combination of VEGETABLES, PROTEINS, STARCH/FRUIT and FAT

OPTIONAL:

2 TABLESPOONS OF DAIRY DRESSING per meal
Up to 9% fat

300ml (½ pint) DAIRY PRODUCTS per day
Up to 3.5% fat
Max. 5g sugars per 100g

READ MORE ABOUT WHAT SHOULD BE IN YOUR HANDFULS ON PAGES 226–243.

THE ONLY RULE IN SCANDI SENSE:
'THE TWO-OUT-OF-THREE PRINCIPLE'

Yogurt and
muesli

**AT LEAST TWO OF THE DAY'S THREE MEALS
SHOULD FOLLOW THE SENSE MEAL-BOX MODEL**

The Sense Meal-Box Model tells you what and how much there should be on your plate: 1–2 handfuls of vegetables, a handful of protein, a handful of starch and/or fruit in the form of bread, pasta, rice, potatoes, berries or the like and, in addition, 1–3 tablespoons of fat. I call this way of dividing up the food the Sense Meal-Box Model.

In addition, you can drink limited amounts of dairy products, as well as freely enjoy drinks with zero calories. However, the best way to quench your thirst is with water.

Scandi Sense doesn't contain a lot of rules. Rules confuse and cause us to lose our motivation and overview. However, there is one rule you should always follow: at least two of your three daily meals should follow the Sense Meal-Box Model.

This rule means that if you don't feel like vegetables in the morning, you can skip them and enjoy some yogurt and muesli or whatever you prefer to eat in the morning. However, you must remember to eat the right combination of vegetables, protein, starch/fruit and fat for lunch and dinner. The starch/fruit portion could be swapped for more vegetables and protein – see how on page 35.

It is important that you keep this balance in mind at all times. Even though you may deviate from the Sense Meal-Box Model with one of your three meal-boxes, make sure you don't eat more food calorie-wise than is in a meal-box.

For example, if you choose to eat a piece of cake, you should be conscious of not putting a lot of additional calories in the same box, because then the balance will be off.

How to measure with your hands

When trying to lose weight, it is important that you include food
in the meal-boxes – and so on your plate – in the right quantities.
Take a look at your hands. If you stretch them out completely, you
will have a large surface area. If you gather your fingers and thumb
together and curve the palm of your hand, you will find the correct
handful size in relation to the Scandi Sense way of thinking.

Then it is simply a question of building a sensibly composed meal
from 3–4 handfuls, with the right proportions of carbohydrates,
protein and fats.

HANDFUL 1 (+2)

HANDFUL 3

HANDFUL 4

1–3 TABLESPOONS
OF FAT

Handful 1 (+2): Vegetables

Handfuls 1 and 2 consist of carbohydrates in the form of vegetables. The bracketed (+2) indicates that you can choose two handfuls of vegetables, if you like, but a single handful will suffice.

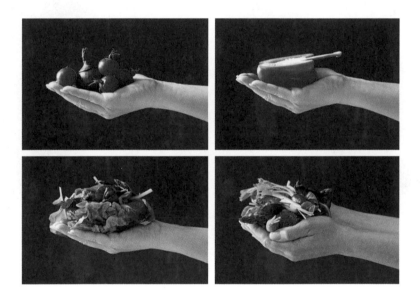

For a detailed list of what can be included in Handful 1 (+2), see page 226.

Handful 3: Protein

Handful 3 is protein from meat, poultry, fish, shellfish, eggs, low-fat cheese or pulses. You must have protein with at least two of your three daily meals, however processed protein (such as ham, salami and bacon) must be limited. If you exercise a lot, it is a good idea to have protein with all three of your daily meals.

For a detailed list of what can be included in Handful 3, see page 228.

Handful 4: Starch and/or fruit

Handful 4 is carbohydrates in the form of bread, breakfast cereals, pasta, rice, potatoes and/or fruit and berries. Handful 4 may be replaced with extra vegetables and up to half a handful of protein if you want to avoid bread, rice, pasta etc.

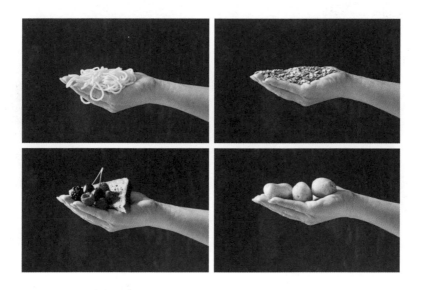

For a detailed list of what can be included in Handful 4, see page 232.

1–3 tablespoons of fat

You can have 1–3 tablespoons of fat at each meal. This
includes products such as olive oil, rapeseed oil, nuts, kernels,
seeds, mayonnaise, tartare sauce, avocado, aioli and pesto, as well
as butter, cream, crème fraîche, fatty cheese and dark chocolate.
Coconut flakes are one example of fat with dietary fibre – the
same applies to avocado, nuts, kernels and seeds.

If you use concentrated fat such as butter, oil and mayonnaise,
eat a level tablespoonful. When it comes to less concentrated
fats such as nuts, avocado, crème fraîche or cheese, you can
eat a heaped tablespoonful.

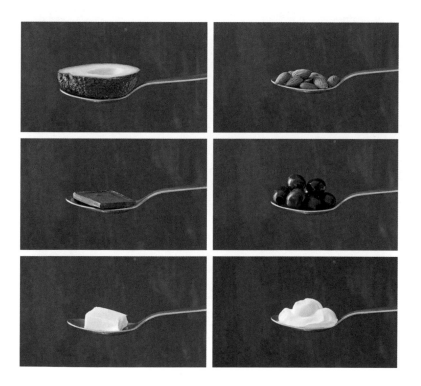

For a detailed list of fats, see page 238.

The Sense Meal-Box Model®

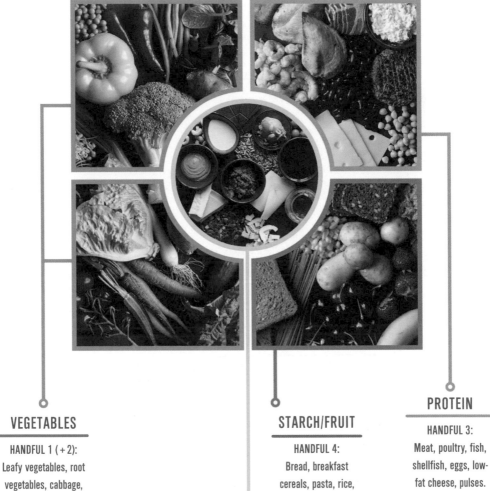

VEGETABLES

HANDFUL 1 (+ 2):
Leafy vegetables, root
vegetables, cabbage,
tomatoes, etc.

FAT

1–3 TABLESPOONS:
Butter, oil, nuts, pesto,
avocado, mayonnaise, fatty
cheese, dark chocolate.

STARCH/FRUIT

HANDFUL 4:
Bread, breakfast
cereals, pasta, rice,
potatoes and/or fruit.

PROTEIN

HANDFUL 3:
Meat, poultry, fish,
shellfish, eggs, low-
fat cheese, pulses.

If you would rather avoid Handful 4, replace it with extra vegetables and up to half a handful of protein. Then the model will look like this:

VEGETABLES

HANDFUL 1 (+ 2)
+ 1/2 HANDFUL VEGETABLES
Leafy vegetables, root
vegetables, cabbage,
tomatoes, etc.

PROTEIN

HANDFUL 3
+ 1/2 HANDFUL PROTEIN
Meat, poultry, fish,
shellfish, eggs, low-fat
cheese, pulses.

FAT

1–3 TABLESPOONS:
Butter, oil, nuts, pesto,
avocado, mayonnaise, fatty
cheese, dark chocolate.

Fruit yogurt

Crème fraîche (can be used as a dressing)

Coconut milk

Cocoa

Skyr

Soya milk

Almond milk

Oat milk

Rice milk

Natural yogurt

Coffee with milk

Skimmed milk

Optional things that you can eat and drink

In addition to what is included in the meal-boxes,
you can have the following:

DAIRY PRODUCTS

You may eat/drink up to 300ml of dairy products a day if you feel
like it – in addition to what is already included in your meal-boxes.
This 300ml must have a fat content of 3.5 per cent or less and
a maximum of 5g of sugars per 100g of product.

For a detailed list of suitable dairy products, see page 243.

DAIRY DRESSINGS

In addition, you can add up to 2 tablespoonfuls of dairy dressing
to each meal-box. The fat content should be 9 per cent or less.

For a detailed list of dairy dressings, see page 243.

Quench your thirst with water.

Drink as much black coffee and tea
(with no milk or sugar) as you like.

Enjoy diet soft drinks as often
as you like, but use your
common sense.

Enjoy alcoholic drinks sensibly.

Drink a moderate amount of
milk only.

Enjoy sugary drinks in limited
quantities.

Drinks

You can drink water, both still and sparkling, as much as needed. Drink 1–1½ litres of water a day – more if you have done physical activity or if it is warm. Black coffee, black tea, diet soft drinks and calorie-free squash can also be consumed as often as you like – but use your common sense.

Decide what habits you want to keep in your life – especially when it comes to beer, wine and spirits. If you want to live a life where there is space for a glass of wine or beer, it is a good idea to establish your habits during the weight loss period so that you have them in place even after your weight loss.

If you only occasionally drink wine or beer and therefore haven't included it in your daily allowance, one way you could compensate for consuming the occasional glass is reducing Handful 4 (bread, rice, pasta, potatoes and fruit) at one meal. This will allow you to balance your calorie intake.

If you enjoy flavoured drinks and cocktails at times, replace sugary drinks such as juice or fizzy drinks with low-calorie products.

For detailed lists of drinks, see pages 244 and 246.

Indulgences

Indulgences is a label that covers different varieties of sugar, sweets, ice cream, cakes, breakfast cereals, crisps, tortilla chips, fast food and sugary drinks.

There are no definitive quantities for this group. If you use a little sugar or honey as part of your cooking, it is only counted as a flavouring. If you eat larger quantities from this category, you should try to compensate for it in your meal-boxes. For example, you could certainly eat a small piece of cake but you should then take away something that corresponds to half a meal-box to compensate. In that way, the majority of what you eat will be sensible food.

For a detailed list of indulgences, see page 245.

Flavourings

Your food should be tasty, so feel free to use different flavourings. This category covers everything that makes the food tasty in small amounts. For the sake of convenience, I have chosen to add raising and thickening agents to this group as well.

For a detailed list of flavourings, see page 247.

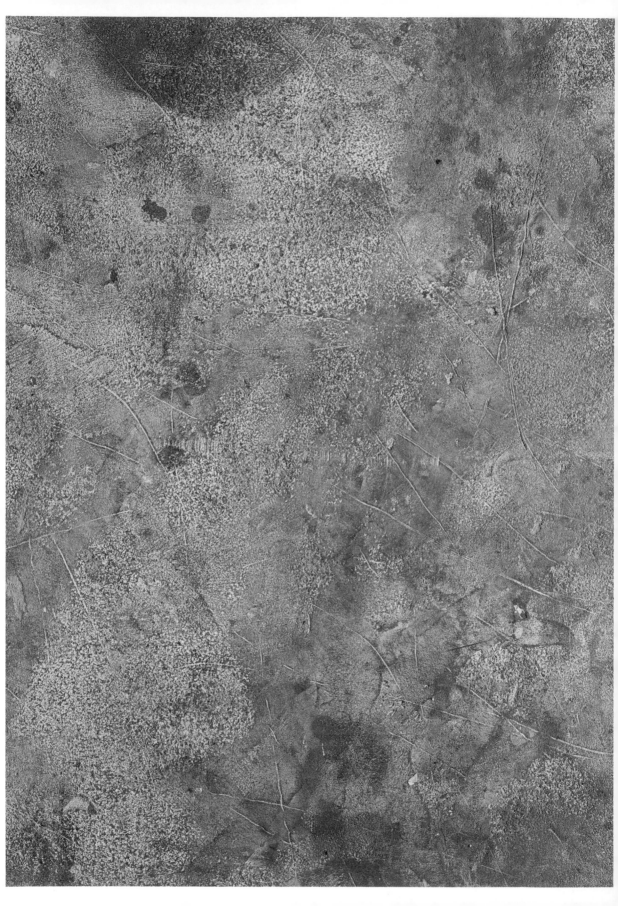

Examples
of meals

Breakfast

If you are in a hurry in the morning and you don't want to eat vegetables so early in the day, you can leave them out and, for example, have regular low-fat yogurt or Skyr yogurt with muesli. You just have to observe the Sense Meal-Box Model for the other meals during the day.

It shouldn't take long to prepare a breakfast that fits the Sense Meal-Box Model. Here is an example. While boiling an egg, gather the remaining items and fill your plate (and therefore your meal-box) with:

Handful 1 (+2):   *Tomato, cucumber, lettuce*

Handful 3*:*   *Eggs, low-fat cheese*

Handful 4*:*   *Crispbread, banana, muesli*

Fat*:*   *Avocado, dark chocolate*

Dairy product*:*   *Natural yogurt*

Dairy dressing*:*   *Two tablespoons crème fraîche, max. 9% fat*

Flavourings*:*   *Salt, pepper, lemon, mint in your tea*

BREAKFAST ACCORDING TO
THE SENSE MEAL-BOX MODEL

Lunch

Lunch is a good time to use leftovers from the previous evening's meal. You can easily put together several kinds of protein as long as it is only a handful in total. The meal should keep you going for 5–6 hours, so it is important to fill up this meal-box.

Handful 1 (+2):	*Green beans, carrots*
Handful 3:	*Tuna, black beans*
Handful 4:	*Rye bread, raspberries*
Fat:	*Mayonnaise, almonds, olives*
Dairy product:	*Milk in your coffee*
Dairy dressing:	*Two tablespoons crème fraîche, max. 9% fat*
Flavourings:	*Salt, pepper, lemon, chives, ketchup in the crème fraîche dressing*

LUNCH ACCORDING TO
THE SENSE MEAL-BOX MODEL

Supper

If you are used to having something sweet with your coffee and are reluctant to go without, it is a smart idea to have it as a dessert at supper instead, as the blood sugar effect is based on the overall meal. In other words, the dietary fibre, fat and proteins in your evening meal can guard against the dessert raising your blood sugar levels.

Handful 1 (+2):   *Mushroom, onion, lettuce*

Handful 3:   *Beef*

Handful 4:   *Potato*

Fat: *Feta cheese, crème fraîche, butter/olive oil for frying*

Dairy dressing: *Two tablespoons crème fraîche, max. 9% fat*

Flavourings: *Salt, pepper, thyme, dill, curry in the dressing, mint in your water*

SUPPER ACCORDING TO
THE SENSE MEAL-BOX MODEL

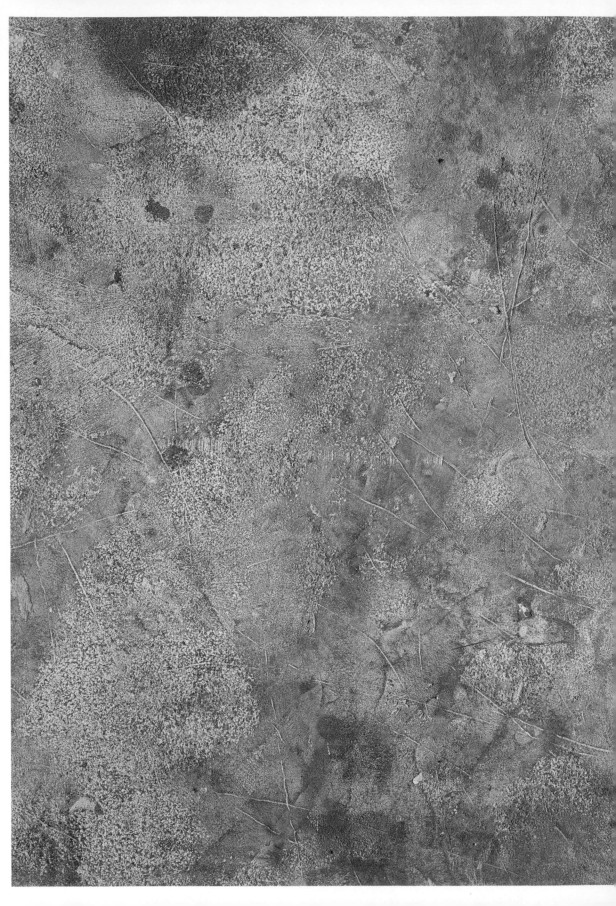

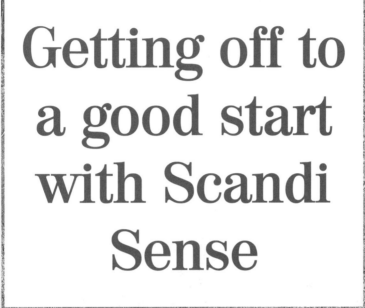

Getting off to a good start with Scandi Sense

I recommend that you follow the Scandi Sense principles completely for the first 14 days; that is, three meal-boxes created following the Sense Meal-Box Model each day. Filling up the meal-boxes completely will make it easier to avoid snacking between meals.

If it is hard for you to wait such a long time between meals, drink a cup of hot bouillon a couple of times a day to counteract any side effects of reducing your carbohydrate intake. You can read more about this in the 'Beginner's difficulties' section on page 56.

I advise you to complete a diet plan for the first 14 days. See an example of a completed diet plan for a woman on page 146 and for a man on page 214. There is an empty chart for you to photocopy and fill in on page 67.

You can start either by following the recipes in this book or by using your current diet as the basis. Just be sure to follow the portion guidelines – handfuls of food and tablespoonfuls of fat. You could easily select one or two favourite breakfasts and alternate between them for the first 14 days, and you can freely choose between all the lunches and suppers.

Look through your assortment of food. Fill the fridge with vegetables. Start using those you are familiar with and know you like – you can always expand your repertoire later. Seasonal vegetables are cheap and full of vitamins, but don't buy more than you can use. Fill the freezer with readily available vegetables such as spinach, peas, beans and so on, so that you never run out of vegetables.

Fresh meat, fish, poultry and cheese are excellent sources of protein. But it is a good idea to stock up on canned fish such as mackerel, cod roe and tuna. Just like a tray of ready-made fishcakes, they are an easy solution for lunch or for a quick meal.

Make sure that you have several different fats in your kitchen: butter, olive oil, mayonnaise, olives, nuts, almonds and fatty cheese.

Choose wholemeal when eating bread. Most people don't eat much fruit at first in Scandi Sense, but it is a good idea to keep berries or berry mixes in the freezer. Keep a litre of milk, a cultured dairy product and, for example, crème fraîche (5–9 per cent) in the fridge, so you are well prepared.

Beginner's difficulties

You won't feel normal during the first 14 days of Scandi Sense. Remember that you are challenging your body to adapt to your new diet. It may well bring with it some reactions, not all of which are fun. The extent of the body's reaction varies enormously.

DIZZY, TIRED AND BESIDE YOURSELF?

Some people experience almost no difficulties when beginning the diet, while others feel as if they have a mild flu, with symptoms such as headaches, dizziness, increased urination, stomach problems (diarrhoea or constipation, for example), low energy levels and irritation.

The symptoms arise because the body is responding to a change of diet. It is natural and you mustn't feel discouraged. You will have to use all your reserves of patience and faith that things will turn around after the first few weeks.

The digestive system can take several weeks to adapt to new dietary habits.

Don't eat too many raw vegetables if you aren't used to them, as they may be difficult for your stomach to handle. Instead, you can fry, boil, roast or steam some of your vegetables.

Drink 1–2 cups of hot bouillon every day for the first few weeks. During the early days of Scandi Sense, you are draining fluids from the body and this can cause discomfort. The salt in bouillon helps to counteract this effect.

DO YOU FIND IT DIFFICULT TO AVOID SNACKS?

Many people eat more out of habit than hunger. It is important that you become familiar with the feeling of hunger using the hunger barometer (see page 21). If you find it difficult to keep hunger at bay with three meals a day, you can do one of two things.

You can add a little more into one of your meal-boxes by, for example, increasing the amount of protein by 5–10 per cent. It may be that you are not getting enough food.

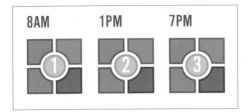

SOLUTION:

Put some extra food – preferably protein – in Meal-Box 1 and/or 2. Or you can take some food from a meal-box and eat it as a snack.

Or, you can divide your allowance between three main meals and one or more snacks. You have to find your own way, even when it comes to the number of meals. Scandi Sense will still work as long as you don't eat more overall than what can be in the suggested three meal-boxes.

If you choose to introduce snacks during the day, it is a good idea to choose a small snack that contains protein, carbohydrate and fat. This combination will fill you up and keep your blood sugar levels stable. Of course you can just eat a carrot or another vegetable, if that's what works for you.

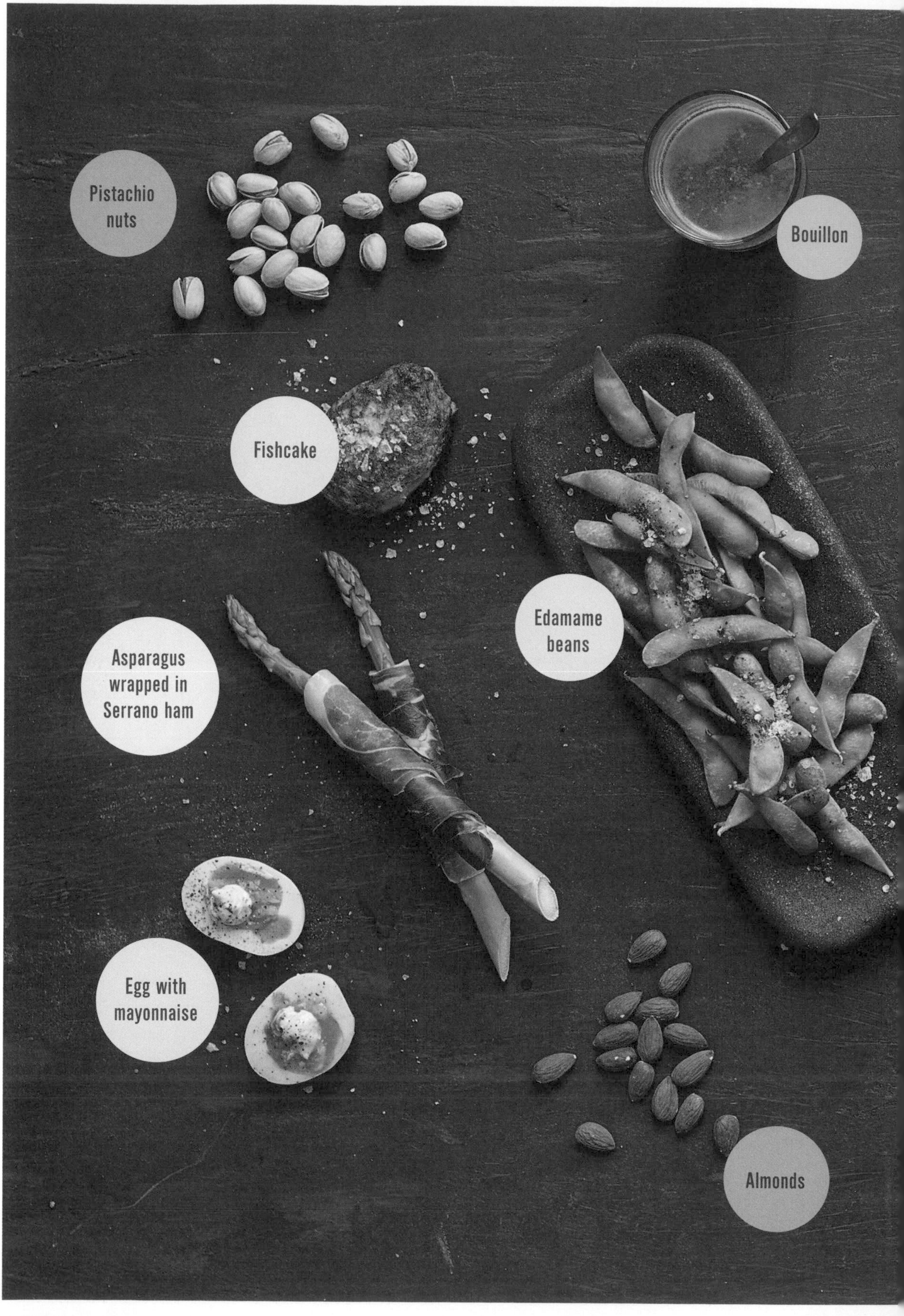

Pistachio nuts

Bouillon

Fishcake

Edamame beans

Asparagus wrapped in Serrano ham

Egg with mayonnaise

Almonds

13
quick
snacks:

SEE THE NEXT PAGE FOR QUANTITIES

Crispbread, cream cheese and ham

Avocado

Lettuce with cottage cheese

Chocolate-covered walnuts

Greek yogurt with chia seeds and berries

Cucumber with prawn salad

TIP
Quick broth: Stir half a bouillon cube in 200–300ml of boiling water.

13 quick snacks: How much you can eat

25 grams of pistachio nuts in their shells

1 tablespoonful of fat. 85 kcal

A cup of bouillon

Can be drunk as necessary, as there are only 13kcal in 300ml of ready-mixed bouillon. You can buy bouillon drinks, but a bouillon cube or a teaspoon of bouillon powder stirred into water is just as good. 13 kcal

A fishcake

Counts as half of Handful 3. 93 kcal

2 spears of asparagus wrapped in Serrano ham

Counts as half of Handful 1 and one third of Handful 3. 45 kcal

150 grams of edamame beans with chilli and salt flakes

Counts as half of Handful 3. 109 kcal

A piece of thin crispbread with a tablespoon of low-fat cream cheese and two slices of ham

Counts as one third of Handful 4 and half of Handful 3. 80 kcal

Half an avocado with a teaspoon of lemon juice, salt and pepper

Counts as 2 tablespoonfuls of fat. 134 kcal

15 almonds

Counts as 1 tablespoonful of fat. 79 kcal

1 hard-boiled egg with 10 grams of mayonnaise, plus tabasco, salt and pepper

Counts as one third of Handful 3 and 1 tablespoonful of fat. 149 kcal

Two baby romaine lettuce leaves with 50 grams of cottage cheese and half a teaspoonful of sunflower seeds

Counts as one quarter of Handful 1, one third of Handful 3 and half a tablespoonful of fat. 96 kcal

Three walnuts dipped in 10 grams of dark chocolate (min. 70%) with a sprinkle of freeze-dried raspberries, liquorice and edible glitter

Counts as 2 tablespoonfuls of fat. 166 kcal

100 grams of cucumber with 25 grams of prawn salad

Counts as Handful 1, one fifth of Handful 3 and 1 tablespoonful of fat. 86 kcal

100 millilitres of 2% Greek yogurt mixed with 15 grams of chia seeds and decorated with 25 grams of berries

Counts as 100ml of dairy product, 1 tablespoonful of fat and one quarter of Handful 4. 156 kcal

What about dining out?

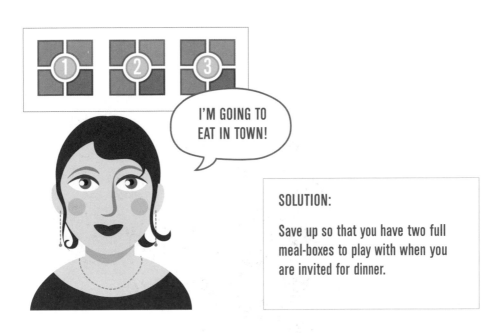

Once you have understood the principles behind the meal-boxes, you can play about with them – for example, if you are eating out or having guests for dinner.

THREE STRATEGIES FOR A BIG MEAL

If you only eat half a meal-box for breakfast and half a meal-box for lunch, you will have two whole meal-boxes to play with for your evening meal.

If you skip either breakfast or lunch completely, you will also have two whole meal-boxes available in the evening.

You can also fill your meal-boxes for breakfast and lunch as normal and complete the last meal-box to the best of your ability. The crucial thing is to be level-headed, do not overeat and be sure to get back into a good rhythm at the next mealtime.

How much exercise do you need?

Exercise is good for your health, your mood, your muscles, your bones and your joints. It can also make it easier for you to maintain a healthy weight when you have lost some weight. But when you reach the point where you want a few extra pounds to disappear, it is predominantly your eating habits that determine whether or not you will succeed.

During an attempt at weight loss, exercise works a bit like stepping on the gas – it speeds it up a little.

However, to be completely honest with you, it doesn't make a great deal of difference.

Fortunately, there are plenty of other good reasons to exercise, and if you have the desire and the energy, I can only encourage you to do so to supplement the Scandi Sense diet.

However, moderate exercise doesn't mean you can eat larger helpings. Some people mistakenly think that they can afford to eat much more because they exercise. Unfortunately, the calorie requirements of the body don't really work like that.

It is also a myth that you should eat both before and after exercise. It is the amount of protein and other macro-nutrients distributed throughout the day that are important for nutrition. As long as you eat a handful of protein two to three times a day, you will get the amount of protein you need to cope with exercise alongside weight loss, as long as we are talking about moderate exercise.

You will only need more food if you exercise a lot, for example, running long distance several times a week or doing intensive weight training for many hours a week. In this case, make sure you eat three handfuls of protein daily – and these can be heaped.

The day before a long run or similar, you can have one or two extra handfuls of starch/fruit. But this only

applies to people who exercise a lot. Moderate exercisers – and that is the majority of us – should be satisfied with the food from the meal-boxes.

I recommend that you stick to the official guidelines for exercise: 30 minutes a day at moderate to high intensity. At least two days a week, you should engage in a heartbeat-raising activity for at least 20 minutes. If you start exercising very long and hard, you risk triggering your hunger hormones, so you will get an intense urge to make up for any weight lost

in exercise with food – if not more. It isn't smart at a stage where you are rediscovering the natural regulation of your appetite.

The best exercise is whatever you feel like doing – and what you can stick to over the long term. It is, of course, fine to be more active for some periods.

Exercise shouldn't stress you out, however. If you are very overweight and are confronted with having to lose weight, it is completely okay to take one project at a time. Begin by taking control of your dietary habits. The desire to exercise often emerges by itself once the pounds begin to tumble off. Maybe you have some pain because of your weight or reduced mobility; this all changes when you start losing weight. You will have less to lug around and you suddenly become able to do a lot that you couldn't do before. As these changes occur, your desire to be more active will automatically increase.

If you feel that you ought to exercise but never really get started because you are constantly encountering obstacles, you need to take a good look at your habits, and perhaps your calendar too. Everyone ought to have time to engage in 10–30 minutes of exercise a few times a week.

Scandi Sense is a lifestyle that can be tailored to everyone: those who are very overweight; those who just have to lose a few pounds; those who don't need to lose weight but just want a healthier lifestyle; those who never exercise; and those who exercise a great deal.

If you don't lose weight

Most people who follow Scandi Sense experience a weight loss of 0.9–1.8lb (400–800g) per week – calculated as an average over the entire weight loss period. If, contrary to expectations, you don't lose any weight, it may be because you are either eating too much, not following the Sense Meal-Box Model or eating too many indulgences.

So try to make your handfuls and tablespoons of fat a bit smaller and stick to your three meal-boxes. Then you will see results. You need to be in a calorie deficit to achieve weight loss.

On the page opposite, there is an empty diet plan that you can photocopy and fill in to plan each meal-box. There is also a measurement chart on page 250 to help you to track your progress.

The diagram on page 22 can be photocopied and pinned to your fridge to remind you of the core principles of Scandi Sense.

Scandi Sense

	MEAL-BOX 1	MEAL-BOX 2	MEAL-BOX 3	
	Handful 1 (+2): Vegetables	Handful 1 (+2): Vegetables	Handful 1 (+2): Vegetables	MOST IMPORTANT ELEMENTS IN THE DIET
	Handful 3: Protein	Handful 3: Protein	Handful 3: Protein	
	Handful 4: Starch and/or fruit	Handful 4: Starch and/or fruit	Handful 4: Starch and/or fruit	
	1–3 tablespoons of fat	1–3 tablespoons of fat	1–3 tablespoons of fat	
	2 tablespoons of dairy dressing	2 tablespoons of dairy dressing	2 tablespoons of dairy dressing	OPTIONAL ELEMENTS
	Dairy products	Dairy products	Dairy products	
Snacks				

Don't worry – you will maintain your new weight

If you have tried out a lot of diets in the past, and have struggled to lose weight, or found that you regain the weight further down the line, you may wonder if it is worth your while to try the Scandi Sense diet. Old failures stick with you, but you are not alone. The statistics show a gloomy picture – after losing weight, almost everyone regains the weight that they have lost, if not a little more. Anyone who has experience with dieting knows that one of the hardest thing to do after a diet is maintain your weight loss.

With Scandi Sense, it doesn't have to be like that because it isn't a temporary diet but a lifestyle that you can easily continue with – so don't let doubt undermine your motivation.

People generally lose a little more weight with Scandi Sense than they initially anticipate. This is because of uncertainty about the transition from the weight loss phase to their sustainable lifestyle. It is of course important that you stick to the Scandi Sense lifestyle after the weight loss period. If you return to old habits, you will quickly regain the weight that you have lost. All that this means is that you must continue to live by the Scandi Sense principles and meal-boxes, and you should try to maintain the habit of eating according to hunger rather than cravings, for the rest of your life.

However, after the weight loss period, there is room for a few more indulgences as long as your weight is stable. You can choose to eat more on a daily basis or you can save up during the week and eat a little more at the weekend. Both these methods are fine as long as you maintain your weight and stick to the Scandi Sense principles.

It may take one or two years before you find the weight where your diet, exercise routine and lifestyle find harmony. I call this the practical ideal

weight because it is determined by the habits you practise in your life. The lifestyle you follow will determine your weight and not vice versa, otherwise you won't maintain your weight.

When you reach your practical ideal weight, it is therefore a matter of deciding – with a view to quality of life – which habits you don't want to go without. Then you must lay out a plan that makes room for them within the Scandi Sense model.

Once you have lost weight, you may panic if the needle on the bathroom scales suddenly moves a little in the wrong direction. It is important to know that a stable body weight regularly fluctuates by 4½–6½lb (2–3kg). Likewise, you must be prepared for the eventuality that, even though you have reached your practical ideal weight, it may change over time. Very few people weigh the same at 50 years old as they did at 20 because the body changes hormonally and metabolically as you age, so you don't need as many calories as you once did. It can be difficult to accept, but it is perfectly normal for your weight to rise slightly in line with age.

Mette and John
The best thing we have ever done

HOW WE LIVED BEFORE SCANDI SENSE

METTE: My spinal cord was damaged in a traffic accident in 1998, so I have trouble walking and use a wheelchair a lot of the time. I live with chronic pain and cannot exercise due to cysts in my spinal cord. The cysts cause me to lose control of my legs if I am overloaded. My life is therefore very sedentary.

Before the accident, I was very active. I loved my job and, with four children in the house, it goes without saying that

I also had an active family life. My physical condition in the years following the car crash has slowly deteriorated, but I didn't receive my final diagnosis, syringomyelia (cysts in my spinal cord) until 2013. Following the diagnosis, I was given early retirement.

The deterioration in my body combined with this final diagnosis made me feel that I had lost my entire identity; everything that had defined me before was suddenly taken away. I could no longer work, I couldn't be very active and I didn't feel I could give my children what I wanted to give them. I fell into a hole and stopped looking after myself.

I took – and still do take – a lot of medication for my illness, which was a contributing factor in my weight gain, but the rest of it was down to diet. I didn't eat a lot of food, but what I did eat was unhealthy. We often had take-away burgers for supper, for example, and if we prepared food ourselves, it was always fried in butter or oil. I only drank coke or coffee, never water. I had very little strength and my life was just about survival, nothing more. This affected what I ate and drank.

When my weight exceeded 207lb (94kg), I started to have more physical problems, such as heart palpitations, and I felt constantly out of sorts. Because of my background in health work, I knew plenty about the connection between an unhealthy diet, excess weight, lack of exercise and blood clots. So, I went to the doctor and had a cardiovascular study that showed that I had high cholesterol and an irregular heartbeat and that I was in the high-risk zone for a blood clot because of my weight and lack of activity.

METTE CHRISTENSEN, 42

- Early retiree,
  previously worked as
  a healthcare assistant
- Married to John
- Has lost 46lb (21kg) with
  Scandi Sense in 9 months

JOHN CHRISTENSEN, 46

- Early retiree, previously
  worked as a press operator
- Married to Mette
- Has lost 132lb (60kg) with
  Scandi Sense in 9 months
- Mette and John have four
  children, aged 21, 19, 16
  and 15 – the youngest two
  live at home

JOHN: When I was in my mid-twenties, I was diagnosed with asthma and received medical treatment for it. I stopped playing football at that point because my asthma made it difficult for me to run. The less active I became, the more weight I gained, and I slowly got heavier and heavier.

In 2009, I was injured at work and was given early retirement. The accident made me even more inactive and I became increasingly overweight. I completely gave up. I was convinced that I would never lose weight, so I ate without restraint, because it didn't seem to matter.

On a typical morning, I would eat 2 or 3 bread rolls with butter or cream cheese, and after that I would continue to eat for the rest of the day, consuming about eight meals a day, all of which were unhealthy. I ate lots of fatty foods, for example in fast food shops I would order 3–4 burgers at a time, and I ate lots of white bread from the supermarket. If I was out shopping, I always bought a chocolate bar on my way out. I never ate vegetables –

I thought they were rabbit food.

When I reached 313lb (142kg), I became severely affected by the weight gain. I sweated and puffed a lot and had difficulty getting around. When Mette and I were intimate, I became very physically uncomfortable. My heart would hammer away, I would sweat and my whole body shook.

That's not how it's supposed to be, so Mette made me go for tests. I went to see the doctor and, after an extensive medical examination, I got miserable results across the board – high blood sugar, and consequently the first signs of diabetes, high cholesterol and high blood pressure. Mette and I were both scared by this.

HOW WE LIVE ACCORDING TO SCANDI SENSE

METTE: Pretty much at the same time I went to be examined by the doctor, I stumbled across Scandi Sense on Facebook. I was curious, began to read about it and watched Suzy's videos. I must have been mentally ready for a change because I immediately thought, yes, I could live with this, because it was straightforward and sensible and I wouldn't have to weigh my food or count calories.

Rules and restrictions don't work for me. On the contrary, they make me overeat. Scandi Sense doesn't restrict or tell me off, which suits me well. Today, I live one hundred per cent according to Scandi Sense. I typically start the day with a bowl of Skyr. For lunch, I eat homemade hummus, carrots, almonds, cottage cheese and home-baked bread. We never buy bread from the baker or the supermarket any more. In the evening, I eat different dishes inspired by Suzy's recipes. I have set aside the coke and coffee for good, and I only drink water, 2–2½ litres a day. I can sometimes be a bit naughty – some nachos with the kids or sweets – but it never takes over. I eat a little, then close the meal-box and move on.

JOHN: Mette introduced me to Scandi Sense. I have tried out different diets in the past and have lost weight. But it's always been a tough fight, where I've been hungry and unhappy. So I already had my guard up when Mette brought a piece of paper with some hands on it and introduced me to Scandi Sense. I couldn't be bothered with yet another unsuccessful attempt at losing weight.

But Mette convinced me by serving up a dish of pork chops, cauliflower and cream sauce from one of Suzy's recipe books. It tasted really good; the plate was packed with good food and I was more than satisfied. Mette told me that I could eat this dish, or something similar, every day and that I could eat three helpings the same size every day. I was sold from that point onwards. We stuck together and made a joint decision to change our lives.

It's the best thing we've ever done. We started very practically, by thoroughly clearing out the kitchen and throwing out anything ill-advised. Today we have nothing unhealthy in our home – the fridge is filled with good, healthy food.

The change of diet quickly paid off. The weight tumbled off me and after nine months on Scandi Sense, the scales showed a loss of 132lb (60kg) – an incredible transformation.

From day one, I have lived one hundred per cent according to Scandi Sense. In the morning, I have porridge with raisins and cinnamon or a bowl of Skyr. The day's other meals are made up of vegetables, meat, eggs, etc.

Since we had both retired early, we lost about 26,000 kroner (£3,000) of our monthly income and had to cut back on all our expenses. In the past, we spent a lot of money buying unhealthy food on impulse. Today, as we are following a diet plan, we buy in large quantities and freeze what we can. Even though the fridge and freezer are full of food, we save 1,000–1,500 kroner (£120–180) each month because we no longer buy impulsively. We've set aside the money we've saved, and for the first time in nine years, we've been able to afford a family holiday. We're going to Croatia with our children and we're looking forward to it immensely.

METTE AND JOHN BEFORE THEIR WEIGHT LOSS

WHY SCANDI SENSE WORKS FOR US

METTE: Scandi Sense works for me because there are no restrictions. In general, if somebody or something tries to restrict me, I become stubborn.

99

It works because it's so easy and uncomplicated, without anything forbidden or restricted.

– METTE AND JOHN

This system is so simple that it captured my attention immediately. At first, I measured all of my food with my hands. I don't need to do that today. I know exactly what I can put on my plate because I've carefully followed the Scandi Sense lifestyle for a long time now.

When we have meals out, I don't have to have special food or avoid the food that other people eat. I just make sure I stick to the amounts. You can always find something suitable for Scandi Sense.

JOHN: Scandi Sense works for me because it's so straightforward and simple. Nothing is forbidden so you don't have to beat yourself up or give up if you occasionally eat something unhealthy. You just close that meal-box and move on.

Following Scandi Sense with Mette has contributed to the fact that it's worked so well, I'm sure of that. We've been able to support and motivate each other all the way through, and that has meant a great deal. We've got a lot of inspiration and support in the Facebook group. It is such a friendly place and we're happy to be part of that community.

HOW THE FAMILY WORKS ON SCANDI SENSE

METTE: Our two children that live at home had to get used to our changed eating habits. They made a fuss at first, but quickly moved past it because the food tastes so good. Neither of them are picky, fortunately. Our son used to be an elite football player and our daughter is also active, so they've always had a good attitude towards exercise and health. Nevertheless, they'd been eating the same unhealthy food as us, so they've certainly become healthier too. For example, they often used to buy food in the school canteen, but they don't do that any more. They take wholemeal rolls with salad and meat to school every day.

JOHN: All things considered, the children have taken it very well. They can see the transformation in their parents and are very proud of us. They've only ever known me as overweight, so that's one big positive change. The other day we heated up some ready-made chicken nuggets and chips in the oven, just to make things easy, and there were no vegetables. When the children saw the meal, they told us that it was boring and uninteresting. We completely agreed, and we ended up throwing it all out, because none of us wanted to eat it. That probably tells you a lot about how the relationship with food has changed for the whole family.

HOW WE TACKLE CHALLENGES

METTE: I haven't on one occasion thought, no, now I can't be bothered any more. The hardest times have been the periods when my weight doesn't budge.

METTE AFTER HER WEIGHT LOSS

stubborn. I was on the verge of giving up and telling myself that I had done enough.

But I'm glad I didn't give up. I adjusted my calorie intake and change started again. Now I've reached my goal.

WHAT SCANDI SENSE HAS MEANT FOR US

METTE: My new eating habits have sparked me back into life. I'm a happier person and my self-esteem has never been better. I've found a good balance and think I look great. Everything has become easier for me – getting up, putting my clothes on, just being able to get around. I'm not under as much strain as I was before. In the past, I was prone to migraines, but since starting Scandi Sense they've disappeared. I'm sure that it is because of the increased intake of vitamins and fluids. My body gets everything that it needs now.

Since my accident, I've had problems with my intestines because they're paralysed. Before changing my diet, I'd have one or two bowel movements per fortnight, even though I was taking laxative medicine. Today, my stomach has more to work with, so it happens two or three times a week, and I've reduced the amount of laxatives I take. That means a lot for my well-being.

I also used to struggle a lot with fluid in my body, both in my legs and in my face. Today, the fluid accumulation has almost gone. There can sometimes be a little in the morning, but it's short-term and has usually gone after an hour.

I've always been stubborn and determined, but after the accident I had a huge identity crisis. My self-esteem was at zero and I couldn't see the point of anything – I completely gave up.

Scandi Sense changed all my negative thinking. When I decided to change my

Then I feel frustrated that nothing has happened. But every time, I say to myself, take it easy, you don't have to achieve all the time. And it works, because soon the scales move again. Today I'm just under 2lb (900g) from being in the 'healthy weight' zone. That was my goal, so it's a big thing for me that I'm almost there.

JOHN: My weight loss went well until I hit my first goal of 198lb (90kg). Then the scales suddenly stopped moving. I really wanted to get down to around 176lb (80kg), but the last 22lb (10kg) were

lifestyle, I rediscovered my fighting spirit. Scandi Sense became my project and my goal and gave me the kick in the pants I needed. In fact, we both feel that Scandi Sense has given us a new chance in life.

JOHN: Scandi Sense has given me a new life. I had always been unconcerned about what people thought and said about me, but I recognize that it was a defence mechanism, because of course I got sad if people made comments about my weight such as 'have you swallowed a beach ball?' or similar. When I went to football with my son, I was embarrassed at being a big, fat Dad. Today, people tell me I look fifteen years younger and I'm proud and walk with my head held high when I'm out with the children. I've gained a lot of confidence from getting to grips with my problems, and it was fantastic that Mette and I could do this together.

My annual check-up with the doctor showed that all my numbers are more than fine – in fact they are like those of a 14-year-old, says my doctor. When you've previously had high numbers across the board, that's a really nice message to get. I feel healthy and I know my body is getting everything it needs.

I can also feel a big change physically. The pain in my ankles and knees has disappeared. I don't have headaches any more and my mood is good. I have lots of energy and I'm considering cancelling our big TV package, because I don't use it much any more.

I get a lot of exercise every day. When I started on Scandi Sense, I also started walking 9–11 miles (15–18 kilometres) a day. Every day, whether it was raining, storming or snowing. Nowadays, I walk 4–6 miles (6–10 kilometres a day). I've become totally addicted to it and wouldn't dream of skipping a day.

And then there's the change of wardrobe. I've gone from size XXXXXL

JOHN AFTER HIS WEIGHT LOSS

down to medium. It's crazy! Suddenly I can buy smart clothes. When we were going to a christening recently, I needed a shirt. My son, who is 6ft (183cm) tall and weighs almost 150lb (68kg), offered me his shirt to borrow and it fitted me without any problems. So I wore it!

Mette's top tips

You must be a hundred per cent motivated. If you are, you'll see it through, but you'll need a lot of patience. There will be ups and downs – it's all part of the journey.

Even if you're on medication and have constant pain, or are in a wheelchair like me, it's still your life and your decisions. You have to stop making excuses and take responsibility for your happiness, regardless of what you're up against. Self-pity only makes it worse. I decided that I didn't want to be an angry, bitter woman because I knew that I would end up alone, with no friends, husband or children around me. That wasn't what I wanted.

Extra energy comes naturally if you are happy and experience success. No matter what life has thrown at me and how much the accident changed my body, I'm still the same person inside. I still have my stubbornness, my fighting spirit and my strong will.

John's top tips

You have to really want it, because if you have the right attitude, you'll keep going, even when it gets difficult. And believe me, it's worth it. I feel that my life has started over and I'm so grateful. I've been living with obesity for twenty years and I'd given up completely. But when I finally decided to do it, I was more determined than I've ever been before in my life.

I can barely describe in words what it has meant to me. I love my family above everything and I have a zest for life that has carried me through. I really feel that I've saved my life and been given a new chance. So my number one tip is to drop the self-pity and find your strength and determination. You can do it if you really want to – I'm living proof of that.

Christa and Camilla
It meant so much that we could take the journey together

HOW WE LIVED BEFORE SCANDI SENSE

CHRISTA: I used to eat an enormous amount of bread and pasta – several large helpings every day. I work at a hotel where there is a breakfast buffet every morning so I would start the day with a couple of rolls with cheese and butter. Then I would continue to eat bread throughout the day and at supper I generally had three helpings, simply because I was hungry – I never felt full.

A typical supper would be meat with gravy or sauce, lots of potatoes or pasta and barely any vegetables. If something tasted good, I'd eat a lot – as much as I wanted. I didn't give much thought to the type of food or the quantity. On the other hand, I've never eaten a lot of snacks or sweets. A couple of times a week I might have some crisps, but not always. My weight problems came from eating too much at meals, and not having a balanced diet.

In August 2015, I gave birth to my son and, for a long time after the birth, I weighed over 220lb (100kg). I wasn't happy about that. I had dresses that didn't fit me any more hanging in the wardrobe and it really upset me to see photos of myself. I could see that I was overweight and I certainly didn't want to look like that.

CAMILLA: I think I've always tried to live healthily – at least periodically. But it

was difficult for me to stick to a healthy lifestyle, because I felt healthy food was so dull. At that time, I thought that all healthy food was fat-free and lacking in taste. So, despite good intentions, I always gave up.

Before Scandi Sense, I ate a very traditional Danish diet – lots of bread for breakfast, three slices of rye bread for lunch and meat with gravy and potatoes for supper. I wasn't a fan of vegetables, so I ate very few. I always snacked during the day as well as having three big main meals, so I was taking in a lot of calories.

CHRISTA AND CAMILLA BEFORE THEIR WEIGHT LOSS

I felt really bad about my weight, so my sister and I, along with a friend, decided that together we would begin a healthier lifestyle. We all started on 4 January 2016. At that point, we weren't following a programme, just using our common sense. We began exercising, thought more about what was in the food we were eating and dropped everything unhealthy – no crisps, cakes and sweets. It worked and I quickly lost 18lb (8kg). At that point, we hadn't heard of Scandi Sense, but when I look back on it now, I can see that we had already adopted the principles of Scandi Sense.

HOW WE LIVE ACCORDING TO SCANDI SENSE

CHRISTA: January 2016 was the starting point for a healthier lifestyle. The combination of exercise and the rejection of all crisps, sweets and cake gave us quick rewards. Then, after six months, my sister stumbled across Scandi Sense and began to eat following those principles.

That sparked my curiosity, even though in the beginning I struggled to understand what was involved.

In October 2016, I followed in my sister's footsteps and started living by the Scandi Sense principles – and that was when my weight loss began to make serious progress. Since then I've been eating three full meals a day, and drastically cut down on bread, pasta and potatoes, with a lot more veg and protein.

Now I usually have Skyr with homemade muesli for breakfast. I do have bread in the morning on occasion, but instead of having two rolls, I make do with one and top it with eggs, vegetables and only a little fat.

For the rest of the day's meals, I make sure I stick closely to the portion sizes recommended by Scandi Sense. I make the dishes that I've always made, but I focus on including a lot more vegetables. I have a simple recipe book and I find inspiration for other new dishes in the Scandi Sense Facebook group.

For me the most radical change was changing my view on fat. In the past,

I connected fat with extra weight around my hips and an unhealthy lifestyle. Today, I stick to Scandi Sense's suggested servings of fat, which means, for example, adding a splash of cream to a sauce. I would never have done that before.

I never snack between meals – I almost always feel full. If I get hungry, I've become good at looking forward to the next meal because I know that I'm going to have something good and filling to eat.

Now that I've got the hang of the principles behind Scandi Sense, I don't stand there measuring food with my hands. I do it by eye and by feel, because I know what my plate should look like. I've got used to keeping things in balance with my Handful 4. I can easily save on bread during the day, so there is room for a few more potatoes for supper. If we're eating out or are on holiday, I also hold back on bread, fruit, pasta etc. during the day, so I have a little more leeway in the evening.

CAMILLA: In July 2016, I stumbled on Scandi Sense on Facebook. I joined the group and began to read what it was all about. It sounded like a lot of what I was already doing. It was good to confirm that I was on the right track and to have a specific concept to follow, because until then I'd mostly been feeling my way. Now I had found a finished package that fitted in so well with everything I was already doing, so it couldn't have been better.

From the very beginning, I've lived completely in accordance with the principles of Scandi Sense. I stick to three meals a day and make sure the portion sizes on my plate are as they should be. I've taken up the habit of drinking a cup of coffee with milk and having a piece of chocolate in the evening – it's nice that there's room for that. Apart from the fact that the chocolate

CHRISTA KEHLET, 31

- Hotel receptionist
- Married, mother of a two-year-old boy
- Camilla's sister
- Has lost 68lb (31kg) with Scandi Sense in a year

CAMILLA HANSEN, 32

- Office worker
- Engaged, mother of a two-year-old boy and a three-year-old girl
- Christa's sister
- Has lost 48½lb (22kg) with Scandi Sense in a year and is 9lb (4kg) from her goal weight

satisfies the desire for something sweet, it's become a moment I look forward to, a moment of pure relaxation.

The transition to Scandi Sense was relatively unproblematic for me because I was already working on a healthier lifestyle. I'd cut down on sugar, so the change wasn't that big. I've never been frightened of fat, yet I felt that I should cut down on fat when I wanted to lose weight, even though in fact it was fat I had been missing when I had previously tried to live healthily. Fat gives a feeling of fullness and adds taste to food, so you feel its loss if you cut it out entirely.

I've followed various diets in the past, such as LCHF (Low Carb High Fat) diet. The food was okay, but it was far too difficult to follow. There were so many rules and things you mustn't have. It can just about work when you're at home, but as soon as you step out the door, it becomes almost impossible to live by.

With Scandi Sense it's totally different, because I can live completely normally.

CHRISTA AFTER HER WEIGHT LOSS

I can eat everything – bread, rice and pasta and even cake. I just have to limit the amount and make sure I have the right quantities on my plate.

WHY SCANDI SENSE WORKS FOR US

CHRISTA: Scandi Sense is so easy to follow. Once you get the hang of the principles, it runs itself. I easily become full, despite the fact that I eat less bread and pasta, and in a much more comfortable way. I feel much less bloated than before.

It's a great relief that I don't have to exercise to follow Scandi Sense. I have a high percentage of body fat and I know that I need exercise. The desire to exercise will probably come by itself, but until it does, it's liberating that I can simply focus on the diet. If I was following a programme that required me to exercise several times a week, I'd never be able to stick to it.

From day one on Scandi Sense, I've been motivated to make results happen. And you have to be motivated and have willpower to keep it up. Breaking your habits requires an effort, especially in the beginning. Going with my sister to weekly weigh-ins with a Scandi Sense consultant, Bodil Cramer in Skanderborg, Denmark, helped a lot to motivate me. Knowing that I'm going to face the scales makes me keep going.

I'm so grateful that my sister introduced me to Scandi Sense and that we could make the journey together. I don't think for a moment that I'd have had such a successful result without her.

CAMILLA: Scandi Sense works for me because it's about using your common sense. It's logical and easy, and it's smart that you literally have your quantities at hand. I don't have to count calories or weigh my food. I just have to reflect and evaluate if the food on my plate looks sensible. It's so straightforward.

My husband is a sailor and is alternately home and away for a fortnight at a time. When I'm alone with our two small children, it's very important that I can live according to Scandi Sense without it being too difficult and without having to leave home in the evening to go to the gym or for a run. That simply wouldn't work for me. I just have to concentrate on the food and it works really well. If we hadn't had children, I'm sure I'd also have exercised more, but as it is now, I'm satisfied with doing a little exercise in the living room in the evening.

HOW THE FAMILY WORKS ON SCANDI SENSE

CHRISTA: There are no problems at all for the family. I make the food I've been making all along, but just make sure there are more vegetables than before. I don't make any special food – all three of us eat the same food. My husband eats more potatoes than I do, and I eat a lot more vegetables than him, but we all serve ourselves from the same dishes.

CAMILLA: I haven't had any complaints about the food, either from my children or my husband. I often eat alone with my children and they eat more or less what I give them. If I am trying to restrict Handful 4 (starch/fruit) I make sure that there is still bread, pasta, rice or potatoes for them. I also give them extra sauce and they can have two helpings if they want.

I put all the food on the table at the same time, so the children don't realize that I'm eating differently to them. And my husband doesn't say anything either about the fact that there are more vegetables on the table. He just eats what he wants and takes a few more potatoes.

I often lie in wait for new dishes to emerge on the Facebook group and have tried some, but I mostly make the same dishes that I've always made, just a Scandi Sense version with lots more vegetables.

HOW WE TACKLE CHALLENGES

CHRISTA: Before Scandi Sense I ate five times a day, so at first it was hard to settle for three meals. I've got used to it now and I never feel hungry. In the beginning, I also found it difficult to find the balance when I was invited out. It's often mostly Handful 4 that is served up when you're at a birthday or a party – bread, pasta, potatoes and rice. Today,

CAMILLA AFTER HER WEIGHT LOSS

I've learnt how to find a balance by cutting down on these foods during the day, so I have more leeway when I eat out. It works fine.

CAMILLA: I think the biggest challenge is to stick to Scandi Sense when we're on holiday and the weekdays aren't running in their usual rhythm. Then I start eating the wrong food and too much of it and maybe drink more wine than ususal. It takes its toll on my weight and sometimes I come home from holiday with a few extra pounds on my hips.

"

We have supported each other along the way and shared it all, both the joys and the frustrations. Making the journey together has been invaluable.

– CHRISTA AND CAMILLA

But actually, it's okay to allow yourself to have a little more fun when you're on holiday. The important thing is just to find your way back into the old rhythm with your good habits. Luckily, for me it happens by itself as soon as we're home again – and then the pounds fall off again just as quickly.

It can be the same at weekends if you don't quite keep a tight rein on yourself. It's okay to allow yourself a glass of wine or something a little yummy, but it mustn't get out of hand and develop into parties every weekend, because that's the way it all goes wrong. Again, it all comes down to simply using your common sense.

WHAT SCANDI SENSE HAS MEANT FOR US

CHRISTA: I have so much more energy and desire to play with my son. And I've become a much happier person. The clothes that hang in the wardrobe now fit me and I don't have to go to the supermarket or the plus-size shops any more to find new clothes. It has meant a lot for my self-esteem that I can buy clothes from any shop. I have gone down four dress sizes and suddenly everything they have on show fits me.

When I look at old pictures of myself, I can see how big I was. Today, it's hard to understand that I looked like that.

I currently weigh almost 55lb (25kg) less today than I did when I fell pregnant.

CAMILLA: I've got a better understanding of how to put food together to feel full. When you come to understand the connection between the different parts of the diet, it's easier to live according to Scandi Sense.

I think a lot about food, but it's in a different way to before. Today I take plenty of time to plan my meals. I make a food plan for one week at a time and buy in large quantities. It's both practical, as I'm alone with the children a lot of time, and beneficial, because I save a lot of money by planning the shopping. I completely avoid all the impulse buys that I made when I went shopping before Scandi Sense.

For a long time after I had my two children, my weight was around 220lb (100kg). At that time, I always wore leggings and big blouses to hide my body and I didn't want to go to clothes shops, because I knew the clothes I liked wouldn't fit me and that made me sad. It's different today. I've gone down three or four dress sizes and now wear size 10–12. It's so nice to be able to go into all kinds of shops and find that the clothes that I could only look at before now fit me. It's worked wonders for both my self-esteem and my energy levels.

Christa's top tips

It's important to fill the meal-boxes so that you stay full. The first two weeks can be difficult if you're changing habits such as indulging in sweet snacks and large helpings. So it's about being determined and sticking to it. Take baby steps – just one meal at a time. Suddenly you get used to it and then it isn't difficult at all.

Once you've got the hang of the principles, you can start trying to save up during the day if you're doing something in the evening.

It's a really good idea to take the journey with someone. It's been invaluable for me to have my sister by my side. At the same time, it has been very motivating for both of us to go to weekly weigh-ins. It has kept us going, so I can only recommend others do that too.

Camilla's top tips

Make sure you religiously follow the rules of Scandi Sense for the first 14 days, and fill your meal-boxes completely. Then you will gradually learn what's best for you and adjust slowly from there. Perhaps you will be satisfied with half of Handful 4 for some of your meals or even just a snack.

I don't think that you have to cut out bread, pasta etc. completely, because when you deny yourself something, it suddenly becomes interesting.

It's a good idea to take before and after pictures of yourself to document your weight loss. I often refer to these and it's a great motivation to see how much has changed. It takes a bit of effort to change your habits at first, so it's largely about focussing on what motivates you.

It's been really nice to have my little sister taking on this project with me. We've always been close so it felt natural to take this journey together. We see each other often and eat together at least once a week, so we've been able to share it all – both the joys and the frustrations. We often take pictures of ourselves and our food and send them to each other. It's both supportive and inspiring.

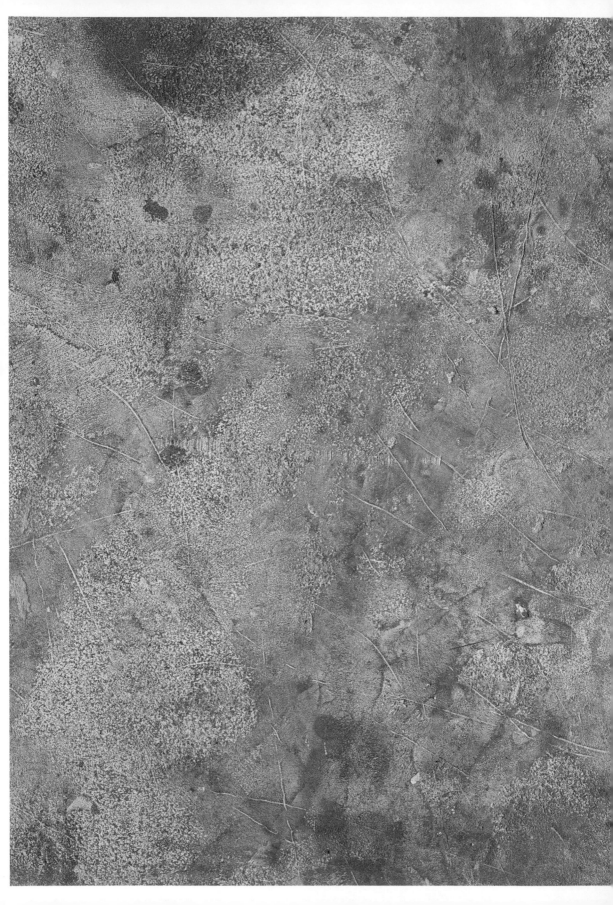

Nine-day
diet plan

Nine days with Scandi Sense, meal by meal

Choose the right diet plan for you

You can start on any day you like, and in principle you can choose breakfast, lunch and supper as you want or need, which you may find helpful on busy days.

If you feel the portion sizes are too large or too small for you, simply adjust the recipes. The idea is that, over time, you will discover how much food you need. You could also choose to have a smaller portion for one of your three daily meals.

If you are a woman, but have a BMI of more than 40, you should probably follow the men's diet plan to ensure that you get enough calories to meet your basic needs. As you lose weight, you will be able to switch to the women's diet plan.

If you are a woman and exercise for more than 10–12 hours a week, again you should follow the men's diet plan.

If you are a man and exercise for more than 10–12 hours a week, you should increase the amount of protein in the recipes or eat an extra half or whole meal-box, divided out across the day.

- RECIPES FOR WOMEN see page 88.
- WOMEN'S DAILY DIET PLAN see page 146.
- RECIPES FOR MEN see page 156.
- MEN'S DAILY DIET PLAN see page 214.

	DAY 1	DAY 2	DAY 3
Breakfast	• Breakfast plate with soft-boiled egg Page 93 (♀) or 161 (♂)	• Toast with ricotta, ham and tomato Page 98 (♀) or 166 (♂)	• Green smoothie Page 105 (♀) or 173 (♂)
Optional snack	• Bouillon drink		
Lunch	• Cottage cheese and mango lunchbox Page 94 (♀) or 162 (♂)	• Chicken pasta salad Page 101 (♀) or 169 (♂)	• Prawn noodle salad Page 106 (♀) or 174 (♂)
Optional snack		• Bouillon drink	
Supper	• Spaghetti and meatballs with courgette Page 97 (♀) or 165 (♂)	• Falafel pita with pesto dressing Page 102 (♀) or 170 (♂)	• Marinated steak with mushrooms and cream Page 109 (♀) or 177 (♂)
Optional snack			• Bouillon drink

	DAY 4	DAY 5	DAY 6
Breakfast	• Toast with salmon and avocado cream Page 110 (♀) or 178 (♂)	• Porridge with stuffed pepper Page 117 (♀) or 185 (♂)	• Pancakes Page 122 (♀) or 190 (♂)
Optional snack	• Bouillon drink	• Bouillon drink	
Lunch	• Buddha bowl Page 113 (♀) or 181 (♂)	• Roast beef wrap Page 118 (♀) or 186 (♂)	• Tuna fishcakes with rye Page 125 (♀) or 193 (♂)
Optional snack			• Bouillon drink
Supper	• Curried chicken and rice soup Page 114 (♀) or 182 (♂)	• Cheesy tortilla tart Page 121 (♀) or 189 (♂)	• Baked sweet potato with chickpeas Page 126 (♀) or 194 (♂)
Optional snack			

	DAY 7	DAY 8	DAY 9
Breakfast	• Breakfast plate with cottage cheese Page 129 (♀) or 197 (♂)	• Ham on toast Page 134 (♀) or 202 (♂)	• Bacon and egg Page 141 (♀) or 209 (♂)
Optional snack			• Bouillon drink
Lunch	• Caesar salad with croutons Page 130 (♀) or 198 (♂)	• Little Gem lettuce wraps Page 137 (♀) or 205 (♂)	• Spinach, egg and chicken wrap Page 142 (♀) or 210 (♂)
Optional snack		• Bouillon drink	
Supper	• Baked salmon with lemon dressing Page 133 (♀) or 201 (♂)	• Homemade burger Page 138 (♀) or 206 (♂)	• Stir-fried duck breast Page 145 (♀) or 213 (♂)
Optional snack	• Bouillon drink		

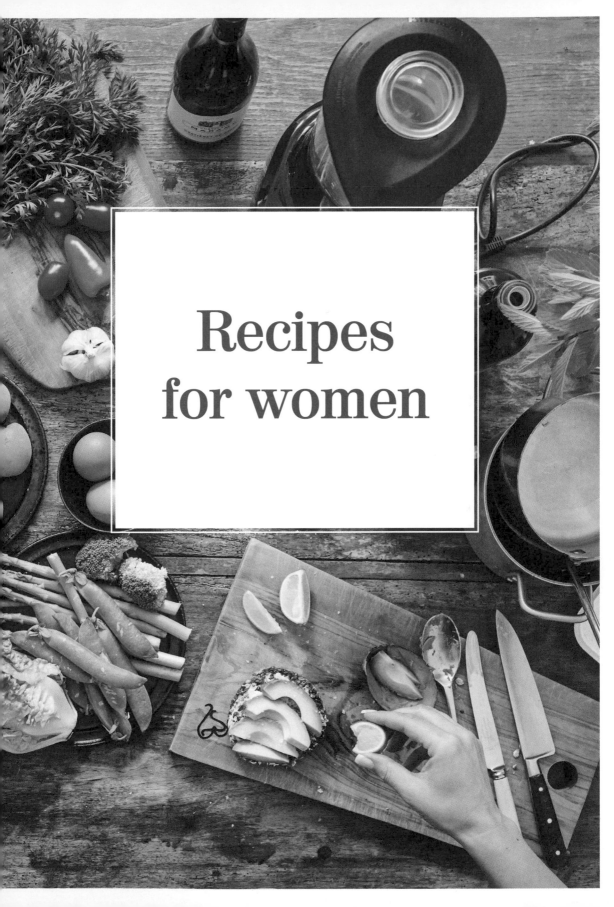

Recipes
for women

Recipes

ALL RECIPES SERVE 1 WOMAN

Breakfast

Lunch

Supper

Breakfast plate with soft-boiled egg

PREPARATION TIME: *about 30 minutes*

BASIC MUESLI:

60g rye flakes
60g spelt flakes
60g oats
2 tablespoons honey
Pinch of salt

PLUS:

1 egg
½ yellow pepper
1 Little Gem lettuce leaf
2 slices of air-dried ham
1 slice of cheese, min. 18% fat
1 piece of crispbread
1 tablespoon jam or marmalade
200ml natural yogurt
15g Basic Muesli
25g berries
15g almonds

To make the Basic Muesli, toast the rye, spelt and oats in a frying pan over a medium heat. When they have browned slightly, stir the honey into the mixture and add the salt. Allow to cool and store in an airtight container.

Boil the egg for 5–6 minutes. Deseed the pepper and place the lettuce inside, with the ham on top.

Place the cheese on the crispbread and top with the jam or marmalade.

Pour the yogurt into a glass or a bowl. Top with the Basic Muesli and berries. Serve the almonds on the side.

WHAT YOU SHOULD HAVE ON YOUR PLATE

Half a pepper with lettuce and ham. A piece of crispbread with cheese and jam or marmalade. A glass or bowl of yogurt with Basic Muesli, berries and almonds. A soft-boiled egg.

HOW IT IS DIVIDED IN THE SCANDI SENSE MEAL-BOX

HANDFUL 1 (+2): *Pepper, lettuce*

HANDFUL 3: *Egg, ham*

HANDFUL 4: *Muesli, crispbread, berries*

FAT: *Cheese, almonds*

DAIRY PRODUCT: *Yogurt*

FLAVOURINGS: *Honey, salt, jam or marmalade*

TIP *The Basic Muesli will keep for 2–3 weeks in an airtight container.*

TIP *You can use shop-bought muesli instead of the Basic Muesli, but make sure that the sugar content does not exceed 13g sugar per 100g of the product.*

TIP *You can use Skyr yogurt or another cultured milk product instead of natural yogurt, but make sure that the sugar content does not exceed 5g sugar per 100g of the product.*

If men are eating with you

Men can have a little more ham, cheese, muesli, berries and almonds. See page 161.

Energy 571kcal · Protein 32g · Carbohydrate 47g · Dietary fibre 5.6g · Fat 28g

Cottage cheese and mango lunchbox

PREPARATION TIME: *about 10 minutes*

150g green beans, topped and tailed
1 tomato
½ red onion
½ mango
15 almonds
50g peas
1 tablespoon green pesto
150g cottage cheese, max. 4.5% fat
Salt and pepper, to taste
1 Little Gem lettuce leaf (optional)
10g dark chocolate, min. 70% cocoa

Boil the green beans for 2–3 minutes. Drain and set aside.

Halve the cooked green beans. Cut the tomato into small pieces and finely chop the red onion. Remove the mango from its skin and cut the flesh into chunks. Roughly chop the almonds.

Combine all of the prepared ingredients in a suitable container, along with the peas.

Mix the pesto and cottage cheese together and season with salt and pepper. Add this dressing on top of your lunchbox, using a lettuce leaf to keep it separate, if you like.

Serve with the dark chocolate on the side.

WHAT YOU SHOULD HAVE ON YOUR PLATE

The contents of one lunchbox and some dark chocolate.

HOW IT IS DIVIDED IN THE SCANDI SENSE MEAL-BOX

HANDFUL 1 (+2): *Green beans, tomato, red onion, peas*

HANDFUL 3: *Cottage cheese*

HANDFUL 4: *Mango*

FAT: *Pesto, almonds, dark chocolate*

FLAVOURINGS: *Salt, pepper*

TIP *If you are vegan, you can the substitute the cottage cheese with pulses.*

TIP *You can prepare this meal the day before and safely store it overnight in the fridge.*

TIP *You may prefer to use fresh vegetables but frozen vegetables are fine.*

TIP *Instead of the almonds, you can use other nuts, grains or seeds.*

If men are eating with you

Men can have more almonds, cottage cheese and dark chocolate. See page 162.

Energy 531kcal · Protein 30g · Carbohydrate 40g · Dietary fibre 13.1g · Fat 26g

Spaghetti and meatballs with courgette

PREPARATION TIME: *about 40 minutes*

TOMATO SAUCE:

2 garlic cloves
½ onion
¼ fresh chilli (optional)
1 teaspoon olive oil
½ teaspoon paprika
½ can chopped tomatoes

Salt and pepper, to taste

MEATBALLS:

150g minced pork and veal, max. 7% fat
1 tablespoon breadcrumbs
1 small egg
½ handful parsley, chopped
1 teaspoon dried oregano
½ teaspoon salt
1 teaspoon olive oil, for frying

TO GO WITH IT:

25g spaghetti, uncooked
½ courgette
20g Parmesan cheese, shaved
Nasturtium flowers or parsley, to garnish

Finely chop the garlic, onion and chilli, if using. Heat the olive oil in a frying pan and cook them for a couple of minutes. Add the paprika and fry for a further minute before adding the tomatoes. Season with salt and pepper. Allow this mixture to simmer while you make the meatballs.

Mix all the meatball ingredients together and form small balls the size of a walnut. Fry the meatballs in olive oil for 10 minutes, shaking the pan now and then so that they brown evenly.

Cook the spaghetti, following the packet instructions.

Cut the courgette into cubes, or shred it, if you'd rather, and add to the tomato sauce 3 minutes before you are ready to serve.

Arrange everything on a dish – first the spaghetti, then the tomato sauce and finally the meatballs. Scatter the Parmesan on top and add your chosen garnish.

WHAT YOU SHOULD HAVE ON YOUR PLATE

Spaghetti, tomato sauce with courgette and meatballs, Parmesan cheese.

HOW IT IS DIVIDED IN THE SCANDI SENSE MEAL-BOX

HANDFUL 1 (+2): *Onion, tomato, courgette*

HANDFUL 3: *Pork and veal, egg*

HANDFUL 4: *Breadcrumbs, spaghetti*

FAT: *Olive oil, Parmesan*

FLAVOURINGS: *Garlic, chilli, paprika, salt, pepper, oregano, nasturtium flowers, parsley*

TIP *You can use only pork or only veal instead of mixed pork and veal. Or combine meat as you like.*

TIP *You can substitute extra courgette for the spaghetti if you want to avoid pasta.*

If men are eating with you

Men may have a little more minced meat, spaghetti and Parmesan. See page 165.

Energy 663kcal · Protein 55g · Carbohydrate 43g · Dietary fibre 10.8g · Fat 29g

Toast with ricotta, ham and tomato

PREPARATION TIME: *about 15 minutes*

RICOTTA MIXTURE:

15g pine nuts
60g ricotta cheese
Salt and pepper, to taste

TO GO WITH IT:

1 egg
1 slice of bread, preferably wholemeal
1 tomato
2 slices of ham
Chives and edible flowers, to garnish
Coffee or tea
50ml milk, if required

Toast the pine nuts in a dry pan over a medium heat. When they are golden brown, chop them finely and allow to cool before mixing them into the ricotta. Season with salt and pepper.

Boil the egg for 5–6 minutes.

Toast the slice of bread and cut it in half. Cut the tomato into slices.

Spread the ricotta mixture on to the bread, then add a slice of ham to each and a couple of slices of tomato. Season with salt and pepper and garnish with chives.

You can drink a cup of tea or coffee with this meal, and add milk if you want to.

WHAT YOU SHOULD HAVE ON YOUR PLATE

Two half slices of bread with topping, a soft-boiled egg and a cup of tea or coffee.

HOW IT IS DIVIDED IN THE SCANDI SENSE MEAL-BOX

HANDFUL 1 (+ 2): *Tomato*

HANDFUL 3: *Ricotta, egg, ham*

HANDFUL 4: *Bread*

FAT: *Pine nuts*

DAIRY PRODUCT: *Milk, if used*

FLAVOURINGS: *Salt, pepper, chives, edible flowers*

TIP *Additionally, there is room for you to eat 10–15 almonds, a piece of dark chocolate or 8–10 olives with this meal.*

If men are eating with you

Men can have an extra egg and a few more pine nuts, more ricotta, bread and ham. See page 166.

Energy 456kcal · Protein 24g · Carbohydrate 30g · Dietary fibre 5.7g · Fat 26g

Chicken pasta salad

PREPARATION TIME: *about 10 minutes*
PLEASE NOTE: *The recipe uses cooked pasta.*

70g frozen edamame beans
2 tablespoons lemon juice
½ small red onion
½ red pepper
½ avocado
10g cashew nuts
25g mixed salad leaves
80g cooked chicken, diced or in strips
75g cooked pasta, preferably wholemeal

YOGURT DRESSING:

1 garlic clove
1 tablespoon chopped chives
50ml natural yogurt
½ teaspoon salt
Sprinkling of pepper
1 tablespoon lemon juice

Place the frozen edamame beans in a bowl and pour over boiling water. Leave for a minute, then drain and toss them in a tablespoon of the lemon juice.

Finely dice the onion and pepper.

Peel and cube the avocado and toss in the remaining lemon juice.

Roughly chop the cashew nuts.

Finely chop the garlic and mix with the rest of the ingredients for the yogurt dressing.

Arrange all the items, including the chicken and pasta, with lettuce, either in a jar or on a plate. Serve the dressing on the side.

WHAT YOU SHOULD HAVE ON YOUR PLATE

A pasta salad with dressing.

HOW IT IS DIVIDED IN THE SCANDI SENSE MEAL-BOX

HANDFUL 1 (+2): *Red onion, pepper, lettuce*

HANDFUL 3: *Edamame beans, chicken*

HANDFUL 4: *Pasta*

FAT: *Avocado, cashew nuts*

DAIRY DRESSING: *Yogurt*

FLAVOURINGS: *Lemon juice, garlic, chives, salt, pepper*

TIP *You can choose other sources of protein instead of the chicken and edamame beans – you can choose freely between other meats, fish, shellfish, low-fat cheese or pulses. You can easily use up leftovers from supper the day before in this way.*

TIP *Instead of the pasta you can substitute rice, sweetcorn, bulgur wheat, couscous, wheat berries, even a piece of baguette – any other carbohydrate item.*

If men are eating with you

Men can have more edamame beans, cashew nuts, chicken and pasta. See page 169.

Energy 579kcal · Protein 36g · Carbohydrate 36g · Dietary fibre 10g · Fat 24g

Falafel pita with pesto dressing

PREPARATION TIME INCLUDING BAKING: *about 45 minutes*

PLEASE NOTE: *It is a good idea to let the chickpea dough rest in the fridge for 2 hours before you form into balls. However, you can make them straight away.*

FALAFELS:

100g canned chickpeas (drained weight)
1 tablespoon lemon juice
½ onion
1 garlic clove
2 tablespoons parsley
½ teaspoon ground coriander
½ teaspoon salt
½ teaspoon cayenne pepper
½ teaspoon ground cumin
1 small egg
1–2 tablespoons plain flour
1 tablespoon olive oil
1 tablespoon breadcrumbs

SALAD:

40g cherry tomatoes
40g peas
30g lamb's lettuce or other salad leaves
Pea shoots (optional)

DRESSING:

2 large tablespoons natural yogurt
   or other low-fat dairy product
1 teaspoon red or green pesto

TO GO WITH IT:

½ pita bread, preferably wholemeal
Lemon wedges

Toss the chickpeas in the lemon juice. Roughly chop the onion, garlic and parsley. Blend in a food processor with the chickpeas. Add the coriander, salt, cayenne pepper, cumin and egg and blend to a coarse consistency.

Add just enough flour, a tablespoon at a time, so the dough is firm enough to roll into walnut-sized balls.

Place the balls on a baking sheet lined with greaseproof paper. Brush them with olive oil, sprinkle with breadcrumbs and turn carefully. Press down lightly on them before brushing with more olive oil and sprinkling with more breadcrumbs. Bake in the middle of an oven preheated to 200ºC, Gas Mark 6 for 30 minutes, turning halfway through.

Arrange the salad, falafel and dressing on top of the pita. Garnish with lemon wedges.

WHAT YOU SHOULD HAVE ON YOUR PLATE

Two handfuls of salad, one handful of falafel, half a pita bread and 2–3 tablespoons of dressing.

HOW IT IS DIVIDED IN THE SCANDI SENSE MEAL-BOX

HANDFUL 1 (+ 2): *Onion, tomato, peas, salad, pea shoots*

HANDFUL 3: *Chickpeas, egg*

HANDFUL 4: *Flour, breadcrumbs, pita bread*

FAT: *Olive oil, pesto*

DAIRY DRESSING: *Yogurt*

FLAVOURINGS: *Lemon juice, garlic, parsley, coriander, salt, cayenne pepper, cumin*

If men are eating with you

Men can have slightly more chickpeas and pita bread. See page 170.

Energy 620kcal · Protein 25g · Carbohydrate 64g · Dietary fibre 15g · Fat 26g

TIPS
*Substitute
a tortilla wrap or
flatbread for the pita
bread. Mix the falafel dough
with a hand blender instead
of in a food processor. There's
nothing wrong with buying
ready-made falafel every
once in a while, when
you're in a hurry.*

TIP
*To make
a vegan smoothie,
use coconut milk,
soya milk, almond milk
or another plant-based
product instead of
cow's milk and
cream.*

Green smoothie

PREPARATION TIME: *about 10 minutes*

100g frozen chopped spinach
150g strawberries, frozen
200ml skimmed milk
60ml whipping cream (38% fat)
½ teaspoon vanilla extract
1 teaspoon liquid sweetener
40g cheese, max. 17% fat
2 slices of smoked saddle of pork
2–3 small carrots
2–3 radishes

Place the spinach, strawberries, skimmed milk, cream, vanilla extract and sweetener in a sturdy blender. Blend everything to a thick consistency. It may be necessary to stop the blender a few times, stir the ingredients and blend again.

Cut the cheese into sticks or small slices. Serve the cheese, the smoked pork and the carrots alongside the smoothie.

WHAT YOU SHOULD HAVE ON YOUR PLATE

A smoothie, half a handful of cheese, radishes, sliced meat and carrots.

HOW IT IS DIVIDED IN THE SCANDI SENSE MEAL-BOX

HANDFUL 1 (+ 2): *Spinach, carrots, radishes*

HANDFUL 3: *Cheese, smoked pork*

HANDFUL 4: *Strawberries*

FAT: *Cream*

DAIRY PRODUCT: *Skimmed milk*

FLAVOURINGS: *Vanilla extract, sweetener*

TIP *Add a little more milk if you want a more liquid smoothie.*

TIP *Substitute an egg for the cheese, if you like.*

If men are eating with you

Men can have a little more cream, cheese, smoked pork and radishes. See page 173.

Energy 506kcal · Protein 28g · Carbohydrate 28g · Dietary fibre 5.8g · Fat 31g

Prawn noodle salad

PREPARATION TIME: *about 15 minutes*

DRESSING:

1 tablespoon soy sauce
15g peanut butter
2 teaspoons honey
Pinch of chilli flakes
1 tablespoon lime juice

SALAD:

40g glass noodles
50g broccoli
1 small carrot
50g bean sprouts
125g prawns
1 tablespoon chopped coriander
15g toasted cashew nuts

PLUS:

Coriander, to garnish

Combine the soy sauce, peanut butter, honey, chilli flakes and lime juice with a whisk to make the dressing.

Cover the glass noodles with boiling water and allow them to stand for 10 minutes. Drain and rinse the noodles in hot water.

Divide the broccoli into small florets and cut the carrot into matchsticks.

Combine the broccoli, carrot and bean sprouts in a bowl. Toss the vegetables in the dressing.

Add the prawns and chopped coriander.

Arrange the vegetables on top of the glass noodles, and sprinkle with the cashew nuts, roughly chopped. Garnish with a sprig of coriander.

WHAT YOU SHOULD HAVE ON YOUR PLATE

Two or three handfuls of noodle salad with prawns, one handful of glass noodles.

HOW IT IS DIVIDED IN THE SCANDI SENSE MEAL-BOX

HANDFUL 1 (+2): *Broccoli, carrot, bean sprouts*

HANDFUL 3: *Prawns*

HANDFUL 4: *Glass noodles*

FAT: *Peanut butter, cashew nuts*

FLAVOURINGS: *Soy sauce, honey, chilli flakes, lime juice, coriander*

If men are eating with you

Men can have slightly more glass noodles, prawns and cashew nuts. See page 174.

Energy 524kcal · Protein 32g · Carbohydrate 61g · Dietary fibre 5.4g · Fat 16g

TIP
*You can use
mint or flat leaf
parsley instead
of coriander.*

TIP
You can use frozen mushrooms and leeks.

Marinated steak with mushrooms and cream

PREPARATION TIME: *about 25 minutes*
PLEASE NOTE: *Marinate the steak for a couple of hours in the fridge, or overnight if possible.*

MARINADE AND MEAT:

1 tablespoon muscovado or soft brown sugar
2 tablespoons soy sauce
½ tablespoon chilli flakes or paprika
Sprinkling of pepper
1 tablespoon olive oil
1 flank steak (about 150g)

MUSHROOM DISH:

2 portobello mushrooms
½ leek
1 teaspoon olive oil
60ml whipping cream (38% fat)
½ vegetable stock cube dissolved in 100ml boiling water
½ tablespoon dried tarragon
Salt and pepper, to taste

TO GO WITH IT:

40g mixed salad leaves
Fresh tarragon, to garnish

DESSERT:

1 passion fruit
1 tablespoon crème fraîche, max. 9% fat
A drop of vanilla extract
A couple of drops of liquid sweetener (optional)
5g dark chocolate, min. 70% cocoa

Mix together the marinade ingredients. Place the steak and marinade in a sandwich bag, close the bag tightly and marinate in the fridge for at least 2 hours.

Slice the mushrooms and leek. Fry the mushrooms in the olive oil for 10 minutes before adding the leek. Add the cream and stock and simmer for 10–15 minutes. Season with tarragon, salt and pepper.

Fry the steak for 6–8 minutes on each side. Allow to rest until the mushroom mix is ready. Arrange slices of steak with the mushroom mix and salad.

Cut the passion fruit in half. Stir the vanilla into the crème fraîche and add sweetener, if using. Serve with a spoonful of vanilla dressing and grate the chocolate on top.

WHAT YOU SHOULD HAVE ON YOUR PLATE

One handful of salad, one handful of the mushroom mix and one handful of steak. One passion fruit with vanilla cream.

HOW IT IS DIVIDED IN THE SCANDI SENSE MEAL-BOX

HANDFUL 1 (+2): *Mushroom, leek, salad*

HANDFUL 3: *Flank steak*

HANDFUL 4: *Passion fruit*

FAT: *Olive oil, cream, dark chocolate*

DAIRY DRESSING: *Crème fraîche*

FLAVOURINGS: *Sugar, soy sauce, chilli flakes, pepper, vegetable stock, tarragon, salt, vanilla, sweetener, if using*

If men are eating with you

Men can have slightly more steak and cream. See page 177.

Energy 566kcal · Protein 42g · Carbohydrate 25g · Dietary fibre 6.7g · Fat 32g

Toast with salmon and avocado cream

PREPARATION TIME: *about 15 minutes*

AVOCADO CREAM:

½ avocado
1 tablespoon crème fraîche, min. 18% fat
1 teaspoon lemon juice
Salt and pepper, to taste

DRESSING:

¼ chilli
1 tablespoon mint leaves
1 tomato
1 tablespoon lemon juice
1 teaspoon white wine vinegar
Salt, to taste

PLUS:

1 slice of bread, preferably wholemeal
60g cucumber
80g smoked salmon
Pepper, to taste
½ handful watercress, pea shoots
   or daisies, to garnish

Mash the avocado with the crème fraîche, lemon juice, salt and pepper.

Deseed the chilli. Finely chop the chilli and mint. Cut the tomato into small cubes. Toss everything in the lemon juice and white wine vinegar. Season with salt.

Toast the bread. Slice the cucumber into long strips.

Spread the avocado cream on to the toast, and place the cucumber and salmon on top. Top with dressing, your chosen garnish and a grinding of pepper.

WHAT YOU SHOULD HAVE ON YOUR PLATE

Bread, avocado cream, cucumber and salmon with dressing.

HOW IT IS DIVIDED IN THE SCANDI SENSE MEAL-BOX

HANDFUL 1 (+ 2): *Tomato, cucumber*

HANDFUL 3: *Smoked salmon*

HANDFUL 4: *Bread*

FAT: *Avocado, crème fraîche*

FLAVOURINGS: *Lemon juice, salt, pepper, mint, chilli, white wine vinegar, watercress, pea shoots or daisies*

TIP *If you are in a hurry, just slice the avocado. Arrange it with the salmon and cucumber on top, with crème fraîche instead of the dressing.*

If men are eating with you

Men may have a little more toast and salmon. See page 178.

Energy 476kcal · Protein 22g · Carbohydrate 34g · Dietary fibre 7.7g · Fat 25g

TIP
It is a good idea to use a combination of cooked and raw vegetables in a Buddha bowl.

Buddha bowl

PREPARATION TIME: *about 15 minutes*

DRESSING:

½ tablespoon tahini
½ tablespoon olive oil
½ garlic clove, crushed
1 tablespoon lemon juice
Pinch of chilli flakes
Pinch of ground cumin

BUDDHA BOWL:

50g broccoli
½ mango
50g red cabbage
65g canned kidney beans (drained weight)
65g canned chickpeas (drained weight)
50g peas
30g black olives
30g beetroot sprouts
10g jalapeños
½ lemon
1 tablespoon sesame seeds

Whisk the tahini, olive oil, garlic, lemon juice, chilli flakes and cumin together to make the dressing.

Cut the broccoli and mango into bite-sized pieces. Finely chop the red cabbage.

Arrange all of the ingredients side by side in a round bowl.

Serve with the dressing on the side.

WHAT YOU SHOULD HAVE ON YOUR PLATE

Three to four handfuls of Buddha bowl salad with three tablespoons of dressing.

HOW IT IS DIVIDED IN THE SCANDI SENSE MEAL-BOX

HANDFUL 1 (+2): *Broccoli, red cabbage, peas*

HANDFUL 3: *Kidney beans, chickpeas*

HANDFUL 4: *Mango*

FAT: *Tahini, olive oil, olives, sesame seeds*

FLAVOURINGS: *Garlic, lemon juice, chilli flakes, cumin, jalapeños*

If men are eating with you

Men can have a little more olive oil, kidney beans, chickpeas and olives. See page 181.

Energy 514kcal · Protein 21g · Carbohydrate 48g · Dietary fibre 19.0g · Fat 22g

Curried chicken and rice soup

PREPARATION TIME: *about 30 minutes*

½ small onion
1 small leek
½ garlic clove
2 teaspoons curry powder
½ teaspoon ground cumin
½ tablespoon olive oil
120g chicken
250ml chicken stock
½ teaspoon dried thyme
1 small tomato
½ red pepper
½ teaspoon salt
Sprinkling of pepper
1½ teaspoons cornflour dissolved
* in 40ml cold water*
25g rice
20ml whipping cream (38% fat)
Parsley and marigolds, to garnish (optional)

Dice the onion and slice the leek and garlic.

Heat the curry powder and cumin in
a heavy-based saucepan until fragrant.

Add the olive oil, onion, leek and garlic,
and fry until the onion has softened.

Dice the chicken and add it to the pan
Brown it on all sides, then add the stock
and thyme. Cover the soup and let it
simmer for about 20 minutes.

Cut the tomato and pepper into cubes
then add to the soup. Season with salt and
pepper, and thicken the soup with the
cornflour mix.

In a separate saucepan, cook the rice
following the packet instructions.

Heat the soup until it is hot through
and add the cream.

Spoon the rice on top and garnish with
sprigs of parsley and marigolds. Serve
immediately.

WHAT YOU SHOULD HAVE ON YOUR PLATE

A portion of soup with rice, garnished with
parsley and marigolds.

HOW IT IS DIVIDED IN
THE SCANDI SENSE MEAL-BOX

HANDFUL 1 (+ 2): *Onion, leek, tomato, pepper*

HANDFUL 3: *Chicken*

HANDFUL 4: *Cornflour, rice*

FAT: *Olive oil, cream*

FLAVOURINGS: *Curry powder, cumin,*
* garlic, stock, thyme, salt, pepper,*
* parsley, marigolds*

If men are eating with you

Men can have a little more olive oil,
chicken, chicken stock, cornflour,
rice and cream. See page 182.

Energy 513kcal · Protein 33g · Carbohydrate 39g · Dietary fibre 6.9g · Fat 24g

TIP
You can substitute the parsley with chives or coriander.

Porridge with stuffed pepper

PREPARATION TIME: *about 15 minutes*

STUFFED PEPPER:

5g pine nuts
½ red pepper
80g ricotta cheese
Salt and pepper, to taste
Cress and sorrel, to garnish

PORRIDGE:

30g oats
200ml water
Pinch of salt
1 egg
10g pecan nuts
10g dark chocolate, min. 70% cocoa
1 teaspoon clear honey

PLUS:

2 gherkins or cornichons

Toast the pine nuts in a dry frying pan over a medium heat. Remove the seeds and white membrane from the pepper. Fill the pepper with ricotta and sprinkle the pine nuts on top. Season with salt and pepper and garnish with cress and sorrel.

Place the oats, water and salt in a heavy-based saucepan. Bring to the boil, stirring continuously for a few minutes, until it has the right consistency. Break the egg into the porridge and stir until it is evenly distributed. Roughly chop the pecan nuts and chocolate.

Serve the porridge with nuts, chocolate and honey, with the stuffed pepper and gherkins on the side.

WHAT YOU SHOULD HAVE ON YOUR PLATE

Half a stuffed pepper, two gherkins and a bowl of porridge.

HOW IT IS DIVIDED IN THE SCANDI SENSE MEAL-BOX

HANDFUL 1 (+2): *Pepper, gherkins*

HANDFUL 3: *Ricotta, egg*

HANDFUL 4: *Oats*

FAT: *Pine nuts, pecan nuts, dark chocolate*

FLAVOURINGS: *Salt, pepper, cress, sorrel, honey*

TIP *You can substitute the ricotta for quark or cottage cheese, if you like.*

TIP *You can substitute the pecan nuts for any other kind of nuts, grains or seeds.*

If men are eating with you

Men can have a few more pine nuts and pecans, a little more ricotta and dark chocolate. See page 185.

Energy 576kcal · Protein 22g · Carbohydrate 47g · Dietary fibre 6.8g · Fat 32g

Roast beef wrap

PREPARATION TIME: *about 10 minutes*

MANGO DRESSING:

20g mango chutney
20g mayonnaise
½ teaspoon curry powder
Salt and pepper, to taste

PLUS:

1 carrot
1 small tortilla, preferably
  wholemeal (about 40–50g)
25g mixed salad leaves
50g mangetout
30g gherkins
120g roast beef, cut into strips or squares
Wild garlic, to garnish (optional)

Mix the mango chutney, mayonnaise and curry powder to make the dressing. Season with salt and pepper.

Cut the carrot into matchsticks.

Lay the tortilla flat on a chopping board and spread half the dressing on it.

Place the salad leaves, vegetables and beef on top, adding the rest of the dressing in the middle. Garnish with wild garlic.

WHAT YOU SHOULD HAVE ON YOUR PLATE

A wrap filled with one handful of vegetables, one handful of meat and some mango dressing.

HOW IT IS DIVIDED IN THE SCANDI SENSE MEAL-BOX

HANDFUL 1 (+ 2): *Salad, carrot, mangetout, gherkin*

HANDFUL 3: *Roast beef*

HANDFUL 4: *Tortilla wrap*

FAT: *Mayonnaise*

FLAVOURINGS: *Mango chutney, curry powder, salt, pepper, wild garlic*

If men are eating with you

Men can have a little more mayonnaise and roast beef, and a larger tortilla. *See page 186.*

Energy 553kcal · Protein 33g · Carbohydrate 48g · Dietary fibre 7.1g · Fat 24g

TIP
*Substitute the
tortilla for rye
bread.*

TIP

Why not make an extra as an easy lunch for tomorrow?

Cheesy tortilla tart

PREPARATION TIME, INCLUDING BAKING TIME: *about 40 minutes*

SPINACH MIXTURE:

½ onion
1 garlic clove
2 spring onions
2 bacon rashers
100g frozen chopped spinach

CHEESE FILLING:

1 egg
125g ricotta cheese
½ teaspoon grated nutmeg
½ teaspoon salt
Sprinkling of pepper
25ml skimmed milk
½ teaspoon olive oil

PLUS:

1 small tortilla, preferably
*   wholemeal, about 40–50g*
20g cheese, max. 18% fat, grated
Pea shoots or nasturtiums, to garnish

Finely chop the onion, garlic and spring onions. Chop the bacon into small pieces, and fry over a medium heat for a few minutes before adding the onion and garlic. Add the spring onions and spinach and continue frying until the spinach has fully defrosted.

Whisk together the egg, ricotta, nutmeg, salt, pepper and milk to make a smooth custard.

Brush a suitable ovenproof dish with the olive oil and place the tortilla in the dish. Press it into the edges.

Put the filling in the tortilla in the following order: half of the spinach mixture, half of the cheese filling, the rest of the spinach mixture, the rest of the cheese filling. Top with the grated cheese.

Bake in an oven preheated to 200°C, Gas Mark 6 for 30 minutes. Garnish with pea shoots or nasturtiums and serve.

WHAT YOU SHOULD HAVE ON YOUR PLATE

A tortilla tart with a little garnish on top.

HOW IT IS DIVIDED IN THE SCANDI SENSE MEAL-BOX

HANDFUL 1 (+2): *Onion, spring onions, spinach*

HANDFUL 3: *Bacon, egg, ricotta*

HANDFUL 4: *Tortilla*

FAT: *Olive oil, cheese*

DAIRY PRODUCT: *Skimmed milk*

FLAVOURINGS: *Garlic, nutmeg, salt, pepper, pea shoots or nasturtiums*

TIP *Season with your favourite herb, for example 1 tablespoon dried thyme.*

If men are eating with you

Men can have a little more spring onion, a larger tortilla and more cheese. See page 189.

Energy 625kcal · Protein 33g · Carbohydrate 34g · Dietary fibre 7g · Fat 37g

Pancakes

PREPARATION TIME, INCLUDING RESTING TIME: *about 30 minutes*

PLEASE NOTE: *This makes enough batter for 4–6 small pancakes, which constitutes 1 portion.*

PANCAKE BATTER:

½ small banana

15g oats

2 eggs

2 egg whites

Pinch of salt

½ teaspoon vanilla extract

½ teaspoon ground cinnamon or cardamom

1 tablespoon honey

PLUS:

5g almonds

10g dark chocolate, min. 70% cocoa

10g butter

4–6 berries of your choice

TO GO WITH IT:

100g sugar snap peas

Pansy flowers, to decorate

Place all the ingredients for the pancake batter in a blender. Blend until smooth, then allow to rest for 10–15 minutes.

Chop the almonds and chocolate into nibs.

Melt a little butter in a pan and drop the batter on in blobs. When they have begun to set, add a berry to the middle of each one. Turn them over when the batter has set completely to cook the other side.

Stack the pancakes with a sprinkling of chocolate and almond nibs on top. Garnish with pansy flowers.

Serve the peas in a glass on the side.

WHAT YOU SHOULD HAVE ON YOUR PLATE

All of the pancakes topped with chocolate and almond nibs. One handful of sugar snap peas on the side.

HOW IT IS DIVIDED IN THE SCANDI SENSE MEAL-BOX

HANDFUL 1 (+ 2): *Sugar snap peas*

HANDFUL 3: *Egg, egg whites*

HANDFUL 4: *Banana, oats, berries*

FAT: *Almonds, butter, dark chocolate*

FLAVOURINGS: *Salt, vanilla extract, cinnamon or cardamom, honey, pansy flowers*

TIP *Use calorie-free sweetener instead of honey, if you want to avoid added sugar.*

If men are eating with you

Men can add an extra egg and a little more banana, oats, almonds, dark chocolate, butter and berries. See page 190.

Energy 576kcal · Protein 30g · Carbohydrate 52g · Dietary fibre 7.1g · Fat 26g

TIP
You can use salmon, cod or other types of fresh fish instead of tuna.

Tuna fishcakes with rye

PREPARATION TIME: *about 30 minutes*

TUNA FISHCAKES:

60g sweet potato, diced
1 can of tuna (about 120g when drained)
1 egg white
1 small garlic clove, crushed
Pinch of chilli flakes
1 tablespoon chopped parsley
1 tablespoon chopped dill
½ teaspoon salt
2 tablespoons breadcrumbs
1 tablespoon olive oil

SALAD:

1 spring onion, sliced
¼ red onion, diced
¼ yellow pepper, diced
25g mixed baby lettuce leaves
2 tablespoons crème fraîche, max. 9% fat

PLUS:

1 slice of rye bread
10g mayonnaise
Nasturtiums or coriander, to garnish

Boil the sweet potato in lightly salted water for about 20 minutes.

Drain and mash the sweet potato. Mix with the tuna, egg white, garlic, chilli, parsley, dill and salt. Form into patties and press them lightly into the breadcrumbs.

Heat a tablespoon of olive oil in a frying pan and fry the fishcakes.

Spread the mayonnaise on the rye bread. Combine the spring onion, red onion, pepper and lettuce leaves in a bowl, and put on top of the rye bread. Place the fishcakes on top and garnish with nasturtiums, or coriander, if you prefer.

Serve the crème fraîche on the side in a small bowl.

WHAT YOU SHOULD HAVE ON YOUR PLATE

One large handful of tuna fishcakes, one handful of mixed salad and two tablespoons of crème fraîche. One handful of rye bread with mayonnaise.

HOW IT IS DIVIDED IN THE SCANDI SENSE MEAL-BOX

HANDFUL 1 (+2): *Sweet potato, lettuce, spring onion, red onion, pepper*

HANDFUL 3: *Tuna, egg white*

HANDFUL 4: *Breadcrumbs, rye bread*

FAT: *Olive oil, mayonnaise*

DAIRY DRESSING: *Crème fraîche*

FLAVOURINGS: *Garlic, chilli flakes, parsley, dill, salt, nasturtiums or coriander*

If men are eating with you

Men can have extra rye bread and mayonnaise. See page 193.

Energy 586kcal · Protein 39g · Carbohydrate 44g · Dietary fibre 8.1g · Fat 27g

Baked sweet potato with chickpeas

PREPARATION TIME, INCLUDING BAKING TIME: *about 1 hour 10 minutes*

1 medium sweet potato
¼ onion
1 garlic clove
¼ red chilli
½ yellow pepper
1 tablespoon olive oil
½ teaspoon ground cumin
½ teaspoon paprika
65g canned chickpeas (drained weight)
½ vegetable stock cube dissolved
    in 50ml boiling water
1 tablespoon lemon juice
1 teaspoon clear honey
½ avocado
40g salad cheese, such as Feta,
    cubed, max. 17% fat

DILL DRESSING:

2 tablespoons chopped dill
2 tablespoons crème fraîche, max. 9% fat
Salt and pepper, to taste

PLUS:

Wild garlic and dill, to garnish

Wrap the potato in foil and bake for an hour in an oven preheated to 200ºC, Gas Mark 6.

Finely chop the onion, garlic and chilli. Dice the pepper.

Heat the olive oil in a hot frying pan and fry the cumin, paprika and chilli for 30 seconds, then add the onion, garlic and pepper. Add the chickpeas after about 3 minutes, let them fry for a further minute, then add the stock. Allow to simmer for a few minutes and turn off the heat.

Combine the lemon juice and honey. Cut the avocado into slices and toss in the lemon juice and honey mix.

Stir the dill into the crème fraîche. Season with salt and pepper.

Unwrap the sweet potato and cut a slit in the top lengthways. Squeeze the potato gently to open it up. Scrape out most of the flesh and mix it with the chickpea mixture. Add the cheese and mix until well combined. Fill the potato generously with the chickpea mixture, then place it under the grill for 3–5 minutes.

Serve with the avocado and dill dressing on top. Garnish with wild garlic and dill.

WHAT YOU SHOULD HAVE ON YOUR PLATE

A filled sweet potato with avocado and dill dressing.

HOW IT IS DIVIDED IN THE SCANDI SENSE MEAL-BOX

HANDFUL 1 (+ 2): *Sweet potato, onion, pepper*

HANDFUL 3: *Chickpeas, cheese*

FAT: *Olive oil, avocado*

DAIRY DRESSING: *Crème fraîche*

FLAVOURINGS: *Garlic, chilli, cumin, paprika, vegetable stock, lemon juice, honey, dill, salt, pepper, wild garlic*

If men are eating with you

Men can have a little more sweet potato and cheese. See page 194.

Energy 613kcal · Protein 16g · Carbohydrate 52g · Dietary fibre 13.8g · Fat 35g

TIP

To make a vegan meal, substitute tofu and soya cream for the cheese and crème fraîche.

Breakfast plate with cottage cheese

PREPARATION TIME: *about 15 minutes*

50g radishes

50g watermelon

YOGURT IN A GLASS:

100ml natural yogurt

10g sunflower seeds

*1 teaspoon clear honey or
  1 tablespoon raisins*

*Red sorrel and rhubarb curls
  (see Tip), to garnish*

TOPPED CRISPBREAD:

½ avocado

1 tablespoon lemon juice

40g air-dried ham

80g cottage cheese, max. 4.5% fat

2 pieces of crispbread

Clean the radishes but leave the tops on.

Cut the watermelon into slices.

Pour the yogurt into a glass or bowl and top with sunflower seeds and honey or raisins. Garnish with red sorrel.

Slice the avocado and sprinkle with the lemon juice.

Divide the ham, avocado and cottage cheese between the pieces of crispbread.

WHAT YOU SHOULD HAVE ON YOUR PLATE

Half a handful of radishes and just under half a handful of melon. A portion of yogurt with topping and a crispbread with ham, avocado and cottage cheese.

> ### HOW IT IS DIVIDED IN
> ### THE SCANDI SENSE MEAL-BOX
>
> HANDFUL 1 (+ 2): *Radishes, rhubarb, if used*
>
> HANDFUL 3: *Ham, cottage cheese*
>
> HANDFUL 4: *Watermelon, crispbread*
>
> FAT: *Sunflower seeds, avocado*
>
> DAIRY PRODUCT: *Yogurt*
>
> FLAVOURINGS: *Honey, lemon juice,
>   red sorrel*

TIP *You can make rhubarb curls when rhubarb is in season by placing thin strips of rhubarb in iced water. They will curl after a few minutes. You can also use them to flavour a jug of water.*

If men are eating with you

Men can have a few more radishes and more watermelon, sunflower seeds, ham, cottage cheese and crispbread. See page 197.

Energy 557kcal · Protein 31g · Carbohydrate 36g · Dietary fibre 7.2g · Fat 31g

Caesar salad with croutons

PREPARATION TIME: *about 20 minutes*

CAESAR DRESSING:

50ml natural yogurt
1 egg yolk
½ garlic clove, crushed
½ teaspoon salt
2 tablespoons white wine vinegar
1 anchovy fillet (optional)

PLUS:

2 Little Gem lettuces
1 tablespoon olive oil
1 slice of bread, preferably wholemeal
Pinch of salt
1 roasted chicken breast (140g), sliced
20g Parmesan cheese, grated
Pepper, to taste
Pea shoots or pansy flowers, to garnish

Whisk the yogurt, egg yolk, garlic, salt and white wine vinegar together to make the dressing. Mash the anchovy fillet, if using, and stir it into the dressing.

Remove and discard the outer leaves of the lettuces and rinse.

Cut one lettuce in half. Brush the cut surface with a little olive oil. Fry the cut surfaces for 1–2 minutes in a hot frying pan.

Brush the bread on both sides with the remaining olive oil, season with a pinch of salt and sauté in a hot pan until crisp on both sides.

Roughly tear the leaves from the second lettuce and spread them out on a plate.

Cut the bread into cubes and scatter over the lettuce leaves. Place the fried halves of lettuce on top. Equally arrange the chicken, Caesar dressing and Parmesan on top. Season with pepper.

WHAT YOU SHOULD HAVE ON YOUR PLATE

Three or four handfuls of Caesar salad with croutons, dressing and Parmesan.

HOW IT IS DIVIDED IN THE SCANDI SENSE MEAL-BOX

HANDFUL 1 (+ 2): *Lettuce*

HANDFUL 3: *Chicken breast, anchovy*

HANDFUL 4: *Bread*

FAT: *Egg yolk, olive oil, Parmesan*

DAIRY PRODUCT: *Yogurt*

FLAVOURINGS: *Garlic, salt, white wine vinegar, pepper, pea shoots or pansy flowers*

TIP *You can also buy ready-made Caesar salad dressing.*

If men are eating with you

Men can have a little more bread, chicken and Parmesan. See page 198.

Energy 594kcal · Protein 48g · Carbohydrate 27g · Dietary fibre 6g · Fat 31g

TIP

Instead of the sauce, you can use 2–3 large tablespoons of ready-made hollandaise sauce.

Baked salmon with lemon dressing

PREPARATION TIME: *about 20 minutes*

BAKED SALMON:

130g salmon
Pinch of coarse salt
½ garlic clove, crushed
1 lemon, sliced

LEMON DRESSING:

20g mayonnaise
50ml natural yogurt
2 teaspoons lemon juice
Pinch of salt

TO GO WITH IT:

100g new potatoes
50g courgette
75g carrot
50g red pepper
1 teaspoon olive oil
Pea shoots, to garnish

Season the salmon with the salt and garlic. Place the lemon slices in the bottom of an ovenproof dish. Place the salmon on top.

Bake the salmon in an oven preheated to 200°C, Gas Mark 6 for about 20 minutes until tender.

Boil the potatoes.

Stir the mayonnaise, yogurt, lemon juice and salt together to make a dressing.

Cut the courgette, carrot and pepper into batons. Stir-fry them in the olive oil.

Serve the salmon with the potatoes, lemon dressing and stir-fried vegetables. Garnish with pea shoots.

WHAT YOU SHOULD HAVE ON YOUR PLATE

One handful of salmon, one to two handfuls of vegetables, one handful of potatoes and about 100ml lemon dressing.

HOW IT IS DIVIDED IN THE SCANDI SENSE MEAL-BOX

HANDFUL 1 (+2): *Courgette, carrot, pepper*

HANDFUL 3: *Salmon*

HANDFUL 4: *Potato*

FAT: *Mayonnaise, olive oil*

DAIRY PRODUCT: *Yogurt*

FLAVOURINGS: *Salt, garlic, lemon juice, pea shoots*

If men are eating with you

Men can have a little more salmon, mayonnaise and potato. See page 201.

Energy 598kcal · Protein 32g · Carbohydrate 29g · Dietary fibre 5.5g · Fat 38g

Ham on toast

PREPARATION TIME: *about 15 minutes*

80g frozen edamame beans
1 tomato
2 slices of onion
60g ham
1 teaspoon butter
1 slice of bread, preferably wholemeal
1 teaspoon mustard
2 slices of cheese, min. 18% fat
1 tablespoon lemon juice
1 teaspoon olive oil
Salt and pepper, to taste
1 handful watercress, to garnish

Soak the edamame beans in boiling water for 30 seconds and drain. Cut the tomato and onion into slices. Fry the ham, onion and edamame beans in butter in a large, non-stick pan.

Toast the bread. Spread with the mustard. Lay the onion and ham on it and place the cheese on top. Place the toast in the pan until the cheese begins to melt.

Place the edamame beans in a small bowl and toss them in the lemon juice and olive oil. Season with salt and pepper.

Arrange the tomato slices on top of the toast. Garnish with watercress.

WHAT YOU SHOULD HAVE ON YOUR PLATE

A slice of toast with ham, cheese and tomato. Edamame beans on the side

---

HOW IT IS DIVIDED IN THE SCANDI SENSE MEAL-BOX

HANDFUL 1 (+ 2): *Tomato, onion*

HANDFUL 3: *Edamame beans, ham*

HANDFUL 4: *Bread*

FAT: *Butter, cheese, olive oil*

FLAVOURINGS: *Mustard, lemon juice, salt, pepper, watercress*

TIP *You can use chickpeas or lentils instead of edamame beans.*

TIP *If you use half the quantity of ham, you can add a fried egg on top.*

If men are eating with you

Men can have a fried egg with this, and a little more onion, ham and butter. See page 202.

Energy 528kcal · Protein 36g · Carbohydrate 31g · Dietary fibre 8.9g · Fat 28g

TIP
You can use up all your leftovers for this recipe. Garnish with lots of fresh herbs.

Little Gem lettuce wraps

PREPARATION TIME: *about 15 minutes*

1 Little Gem lettuce

ROAST BEEF TOPPING:

25g carrot
25g yellow pepper
25g gherkins
10g mayonnaise
1 teaspoon shredded horseradish
 or chopped garlic
Salt and pepper, to taste
3 slices of roast beef

PRAWN TOPPING:

1 teaspoon sweet chilli sauce or paprika
10g mayonnaise
Salt and pepper, to taste
60g prawns

CHICKEN TOPPING:

10g mayonnaise
1 teaspoon mango chutney or curry powder
Salt and pepper, to taste
50g cooked chicken, diced or in strips

COTTAGE CHEESE TOPPING:

50g cottage cheese, max. 4.5% fat
25g peas
Salt and pepper, to taste

PLUS:

Fresh herbs, to garnish
100g watermelon

Separate the lettuce leaves and lay them on a plate to form four small 'bowls'.

Cut the carrot, pepper and gherkin into matchsticks. Mix the mayonnaise with the horseradish or garlic and season with salt and pepper. Roll the beef slices around small piles of vegetable matchsticks, adding a little horseradish dressing before rolling. Place on to one lettuce bowl.

Add sweet chilli sauce or paprika to the mayonnaise and season with salt and pepper. Place the prawns with the dressing on to another lettuce bowl.

Mix the mayonnaise with the mango chutney and season with salt and pepper. Place the chicken with the dressing on to a lettuce bowl.

Top the final lettuce bowl with cottage cheese and peas. Season with salt, pepper and fresh herbs. Serve the watermelon on the side.

WHAT YOU SHOULD HAVE ON YOUR PLATE

Four lettuce bowls with toppings. Watermelon on the side.

HOW IT IS DIVIDED IN THE SCANDI SENSE MEAL-BOX

HANDFUL 1 (+ 2): *Lettuce, carrot, pepper, gherkins, peas*

HANDFUL 3: *Roast beef, prawns, chicken, cottage cheese*

HANDFUL 4: *Watermelon*

FAT: *Mayonnaise*

FLAVOURINGS: *Horseradish or garlic, salt, pepper, chilli sauce, mango chutney or curry powder, herbs*

If men are eating with you

Men may have slightly more mayonnaise, roast beef, prawns, chicken and cottage cheese. See page 205.

Energy 564kcal · Protein 36g · Carbohydrate 30g · Dietary fibre 6.1g · Fat 32g

Homemade burger

PREPARATION TIME: *about 25 minutes*

CUCUMBER SALAD:

¼ cucumber or 1 baby cucumber
2 tablespoons white wine vinegar
½ teaspoon sugar
Salt and pepper, to taste

BURGER FILLING:

2 slices of tomato
2 slices of red onion
50g red cabbage or other type of cabbage
120g minced beef, max. 7% fat
1 bacon rasher
1 slice of cheese, min. 18% fat
1 small burger bun, about 50–60g,
  preferably wholemeal
10g mayonnaise

CREME FRAICHE DRESSING:

1 tablespoon crème fraîche, max. 9% fat
1 tablespoon tomato ketchup
½ teaspoon paprika

PLUS:

A nasturtium flower, to garnish (optional)

Shred the cucumber into long, thin strips and place them in a bowl of boiling water for about 10 minutes.

Slice the tomato and onion.

Shred the red cabbage very finely – use a mandoline if you have one, but take care not to cut your fingers.

Form the meat into a large, flat patty with your hands. Fry the bacon in a non-stick pan, and when it is cooked, fry the beef patty in the same pan over a high heat for a couple of minutes on each side. Drain the bacon on kitchen paper.

Place the cheese on the beef patty and the bacon on top of that.

Drain the cucumber thoroughly in a sieve. Mix the vinegar, sugar, salt and pepper, and toss the cucumber in the marinade.

Warm the burger bun. Mix all of the ingredients for the crème fraîche dressing.

Spread crème fraîche dressing on the bottom half of the burger bun and spread mayonnaise on the top half. Place the cabbage on the bottom half, followed by the patty, then tomato and onion slices and finally the cucumber salad. Close the burger. Garnish with a nasturtium flower, if you like.

WHAT YOU SHOULD HAVE ON YOUR PLATE
A burger.

HOW IT IS DIVIDED IN THE SCANDI SENSE MEAL-BOX

HANDFUL 1 (+ 2): *Cucumber, tomato, red onion, red cabbage*

HANDFUL 3: *Beef, bacon*

HANDFUL 4: *Burger bun*

FAT: *Mayonnaise, cheese*

DAIRY DRESSING: *Crème fraîche*

FLAVOURINGS: *White wine vinegar, sugar, salt, pepper, tomato ketchup, paprika, nasturtium flower*

If men are eating with you
Men can have a little more minced meat, burger bun and mayonnaise. *See page 206.*

Energy 602kcal · Protein 41g · Carbohydrate 45g · Dietary fibre 6.4g · Fat 26g

TIP
*You can use half
a large burger bun
instead of a small one.
Alternatively, you can save
handful number four of one
of the other meal-boxes
during the day – and then
you can eat a whole
large burger bun.*

Bacon and egg

PREPARATION TIME: *about 15 minutes*

1 bacon rasher
150g mushrooms
1 tomato
1 egg
1 teaspoon butter
Salt and pepper, to taste

BEANS ON TOAST:

½ can of baked beans (210g)
½ slice of bread, preferably wholemeal

YOGURT IN A GLASS:

100ml natural yogurt
5g hazelnuts
50g raspberries
Sweet William (petals only) and
    pansy flowers, to decorate

Fry the bacon until crisp in a non-stick frying pan. Place it on kitchen paper to soak up the excess grease.

Quarter the mushrooms and fry in the same pan, until they darken. Thickly slice the tomato. Let the mushrooms rest at one side of the pan while you fry the tomato and egg in butter on the other side. Season with salt and pepper.

Heat the baked beans in a small saucepan or in the microwave. Toast the bread.

Pour the yogurt into a glass or a bowl. Cut the hazelnuts in half and sprinkle them over the yogurt with the raspberries. Decorate with edible flowers.

WHAT YOU SHOULD HAVE ON YOUR PLATE

Two handfuls of tomato and mushroom, a bacon rasher, a fried egg, baked beans on toast and a portion of yogurt with nuts and raspberries.

HOW IT IS DIVIDED IN THE SCANDI SENSE MEAL-BOX

HANDFUL 1 (+ 2): *Mushrooms, tomato*

HANDFUL 3: *Bacon, egg, baked beans*

HANDFUL 4: *Bread, raspberries*

FAT: *Butter, hazelnuts*

DAIRY PRODUCT: *Yogurt*

FLAVOURINGS: *Salt, pepper, sweet William (petals only), pansy flower*

TIP *Not keen on baked beans? Have an extra fried egg instead.*

TIP *Try toasting the hazelnuts to get more flavour from them. A little pinch of salt gives the taste an extra edge.*

TIP *You could add 20g olives to this meal.*

If men are eating with you

Men can have an extra egg and a little more bacon and mushrooms. See page 209.

Energy 573kcal · Protein 31g · Carbohydrate 55g · Dietary fibre 21.8g · Fat 21g

Spinach, egg and chicken wrap

PREPARATION TIME: *about 15 minutes*

SCRAMBLED EGG:

1 egg
1 egg white
1 tablespoon whipping cream (38% fat)
Salt and pepper, to taste

PLUS:

1 tortilla, about 40–50g,
  preferably wholemeal
30g cream cheese, min. 18% fat
25g fresh spinach
100g cherry tomatoes, halved
80g cooked chicken, cubed
10g pine nuts
Marigolds, to garnish (optional)

Whisk the egg, egg whites and cream together. Season with salt and pepper.

Pour the egg on to a hot pan and cook, stirring a little now and then, until it has set. Take the pan off the heat.

Spread the cream cheese on to the tortilla and scatter the spinach leaves on top.

Top with the scrambled egg, cherry tomatoes, chicken and pine nuts. You can toast the pine nuts if you like. Garnish with marigolds, if you like.

WHAT YOU SHOULD HAVE ON YOUR PLATE

A tortilla wrap with two tablespoons of cream cheese, one handful of vegetables, a portion of scrambled egg, half a handful of chicken and a small tablespoon of pine nuts.

HOW IT IS DIVIDED IN THE SCANDI SENSE MEAL-BOX

HANDFUL 1 (+2): *Spinach, cherry tomatoes*

HANDFUL 3: *Chicken, egg, egg white*

HANDFUL 4: *Tortilla wrap*

FAT: *Cream cheese, pine nuts, cream*

FLAVOURINGS: *Salt, pepper, marigolds*

TIP *Add a good sprinkling of fresh herbs to the wrap, such as chives or basil.*

If men are eating with you

Men can have an extra egg and a little more tortilla, chicken and pine nuts. See page 210.

Energy 525kcal · Protein 40g · Carbohydrate 30g · Dietary fibre 5.8g · Fat 26g

Stir-fried duck breast

PREPARATION TIME: *about 25 minutes*

STIR-FRY:

140g duck breast, thinly sliced
½ tablespoon olive oil
100g oyster mushrooms
100g broccoli
2 spring onions
½ garlic clove
¼ chilli
1cm fresh root ginger
50g bean sprouts
1 tablespoon teriyaki sauce
1 teaspoon chicken stock powder
200ml water
10g cashew nuts

TO GO WITH IT:

30g glass noodles
Sorrel flowers and wild garlic, to garnish

Brown the duck well in the olive oil in a hot wok. Remove from the pan and set aside.

Cut the mushrooms, broccoli and spring onions into small pieces and brown them quickly on all sides.

Thinly slice the garlic, chilli, ginger and bean sprouts. Add them to the wok with the teriyaki sauce, stock powder and water. Return the duck to the wok and heat through thoroughly.

Toast the cashew nuts and sprinkle them over the dish.

Boil the glass noodles in lightly salted water and serve them with the stir fry. Garnish with sorrel flowers and wild garlic.

WHAT YOU SHOULD HAVE ON YOUR PLATE

Three handfuls of stir fry and one handful of glass noodles.

HOW IT IS DIVIDED IN THE SCANDI SENSE MEAL-BOX

HANDFUL 1 (+2): *Oyster mushrooms, broccoli, spring onions, bean sprouts*

HANDFUL 3: *Duck breast*

HANDFUL 4: *Glass noodles*

FAT: *Olive oil, cashew nuts*

FLAVOURINGS: *Garlic, chilli, ginger, teriyaki sauce, stock powder, sorrel flowers, wild garlic*

TIP *Thicken the sauce with a little cornflour dissolved in cold water.*

TIP *You can use turkey or chicken instead of duck.*

TIP *Combine the glass noodles with the stir fry while it is still in the wok.*

If men are eating with you

Men can have a little more duck breast, olive oil, cashew nuts and glass noodles. See page 213.

Energy 545kcal · Protein 42g · Carbohydrate 48g · Dietary fibre 7.5g · Fat 19g

Women's daily diet plan

For those who want to plan

Completed nine-day diet plan – see page 87.

Handful 1 (+2):

Vegetables.

The bracketed (+2) means you can choose to have two handfuls of vegetables, but one is enough.

Handful 3:

Protein from meat, fish, eggs, poultry, low-fat cheese, pulses etc.

Handful 4:

Carbohydrates/starch from bread, pasta, rice, potatoes etc. as well as fruit.

Fat:

A tablespoon of fat weighs 10–30g, depending on how energy-packed the food item is. A tablespoon of butter weighs about 10g, and a tablespoon of avocado weighs about 30g.

Dairy product:

Milk and cultured milk products with up to 3.5% fat and 5g sugar per 100g.

Dairy dressing:

Dairy products with up to 9% fat.

Flavourings:

Spices, seasonings and herbs, and indulgences used in small quantities to add flavour to the food.

Day 1, woman – total 1765kcal

	MEAL-BOX 1: 571KCAL Breakfast plate with soft-boiled egg	MEAL-BOX 2: 531KCAL Cottage cheese and mango lunchbox	MEAL-BOX 3: 663KCAL Spaghetti and meatballs with courgette
MOST IMPORTANT ELEMENTS IN THE DIET	**Handful 1 (+2):** · Yellow pepper	**Handful 1 (+2):** · Green beans · Tomato · Red onion · Peas	**Handful 1 (+2):** · Onion · Tomato · Courgette
	Handful 3: · 1 egg · 2 slices of air-dried ham	**Handful 3:** · 150g cottage cheese, max. 4.5% fat	**Handful 3:** · 150g minced pork and veal · 1 small egg
	Handful 4: · 15g basic muesli · 1 piece of crispbread · 25g berries	**Handful 4:** · ½ mango	**Handful 4:** · 1 tablespoon breadcrumbs · 25g spaghetti
	Fat: · 1 slice of cheese, min. 18% fat · 15 almonds	**Fat:** · 1 tablespoon green pesto · 15 almonds · 10g dark chocolate	**Fat:** · 2 teaspoons olive oil · 20g Parmesan cheese
OPTIONAL	**Dairy product:** · 200ml natural yogurt	**Dairy product:** –	**Dairy product:** –
	Dairy dressing: –	**Dairy dressing:** –	**Dairy dressing:** –
UNRESTRICTED IN SMALL QUANTITIES	**Flavourings:** · Honey · Salt · Jam or marmalade	**Flavourings:** · Salt · Pepper	**Flavourings:** · Garlic · Chilli · Paprika · Salt · Pepper · Parsley · Oregano · Nasturtium flowers
Optional snack between meals: Bouillon drink			

Day 2, woman – total 1655kcal

	MEAL-BOX 1: 456KCAL Toast with ricotta, ham and tomato	MEAL-BOX 2: 579KCAL Chicken pasta salad	MEAL-BOX 3: 620KCAL Falafel pita with pesto dressing
MOST IMPORTANT ELEMENTS IN THE DIET	Handful 1 (+2): · Tomato	Handful 1 (+2): · Red onion · Red pepper · Mixed salad	Handful 1 (+2): · Onion · Tomato · Peas · Lettuce
	Handful 3: · 60g ricotta cheese · 1 egg · 2 slices of ham	Handful 3: · 70g edamame beans · 80g chicken, diced or in strips	Handful 3: · 100g chickpeas · 1 small egg
	Handful 4: · 1 slice of bread	Handful 4: · 75g cooked pasta	Handful 4: · 1–2 tablespoons flour · 1 tablespoon breadcrumbs · ½ pita bread
	Fat: · 15g pine nuts	Fat: · ½ avocado · 10g cashew nuts	Fat: · 1 tablespoon olive oil · 1 teaspoon pesto
OPTIONAL	Dairy product: · 50ml milk, if required	Dairy product: –	Dairy product: –
	Dairy dressing: –	Dairy dressing: · 50ml natural yogurt	Dairy dressing: · 2 tablespoons natural yogurt
UNRESTRICTED IN SMALL QUANTITIES	Flavourings: · Salt · Pepper · Chives	Flavourings: · Lemon juice · Chives · Garlic · Salt · Pepper	Flavourings: · Lemon juice · Garlic · Parsley · Coriander · Salt · Cayenne pepper · Cumin
Optional snack between meals: Bouillon drink			

Day 3, woman – total 1596kcal

	MEAL-BOX 1: 506KCAL Green smoothie	MEAL-BOX 2: 524KCAL Prawn noodle salad	MEAL-BOX 3: 566KCAL Marinated steak with mushrooms and cream
MOST IMPORTANT ELEMENTS IN THE DIET	**Handful 1 (+2):** · Spinach · Carrot · Radishes	**Handful 1 (+2):** · Broccoli · Carrot · Bean sprouts	**Handful 1 (+2):** · Mushroom · Leek · Mixed salad
	Handful 3: · 40g cheese, max. 17% fat · 2 slices of smoked saddle of pork	**Handful 3:** · 125g prawns	**Handful 3:** · 150g flank steak
	Handful 4: · 150g strawberries	**Handful 4:** · 40g glass noodles	**Handful 4:** · 1 passion fruit
	Fat: · 60ml cream (38% fat)	**Fat:** · 15g peanut butter · 15g cashew nuts	**Fat:** · 1 tablespoon olive oil · 60ml cream (38% fat) · 5g dark chocolate
OPTIONAL	**Dairy product:** · 200ml skimmed milk	**Dairy product:** –	**Dairy product:** –
	Dairy dressing: –	**Dairy dressing:** –	**Dairy dressing:** · 1 tablespoon crème fraîche, max. 9% fat
UNRESTRICTED IN SMALL QUANTITIES	**Flavourings:** · Vanilla extract · Sweetener	**Flavourings:** · Soy sauce · Honey · Chilli flakes · Lime juice · Coriander	**Flavourings:** · Muscovado sugar · Soy sauce · Chilli flakes or paprika · Pepper · Vegetable stock · Tarragon · Salt · Vanilla extract · Sweetener
	Optional snack between meals: Bouillon drink		

Day 4, woman – total 1503kcal

	MEAL-BOX 1: 476KCAL Toast with salmon and avocado cream	MEAL-BOX 2: 514KCAL Buddha bowl	MEAL-BOX 3: 513KCAL Curried chicken and rice soup
MOST IMPORTANT ELEMENTS IN THE DIET	**Handful 1 (+2):** • Tomato • Cucumber	**Handful 1 (+2):** • Broccoli • Red cabbage • Peas	**Handful 1 (+2):** • Onion • Leek • Tomato • Red pepper
	Handful 3: • 80g smoked salmon	**Handful 3:** • 65g kidney beans • 65g chickpeas	**Handful 3:** • 120g chicken
	Handful 4: • 1 slice of bread	**Handful 4:** • ½ mango	**Handful 4:** • Cornflour • 25g rice
	Fat: • ½ avocado • 1 tablespoon crème fraîche, min. 18% fat	**Fat:** • ½ tablespoon tahini • ½ tablespoon olive oil • 30g black olives • 1 tablespoon sesame seeds	**Fat:** • ½ tablespoon olive oil • 20ml cream (38% fat)
OPTIONAL	**Dairy product:** -	**Dairy product:** -	**Dairy product:** -
	Dairy dressing: -	**Dairy dressing:** -	**Dairy dressing:** -
UNRESTRICTED IN SMALL QUANTITIES	**Flavourings:** • Lemon juice • Salt • Pepper • Mint • Chilli • White wine vinegar • Watercress • Pea shoots • Daisies	**Flavourings:** • Garlic • Lemon juice • Chilli flakes • Cumin • Beetroot sprouts • Jalapeños	**Flavourings:** • Curry powder • Cumin • Garlic • Stock • Thyme • Salt • Pepper • Parsley • Marigolds
Optional snack between meals: Bouillon drink			

Day 5, woman – total 1734kcal

	MEAL-BOX 1: 576KCAL Porridge with stuffed pepper	MEAL-BOX 2: 533KCAL Roast beef wrap	MEAL-BOX 3: 625KCAL Cheesy tortilla tart
MOST IMPORTANT ELEMENTS IN THE DIET	**Handful 1 (+2):** · Red pepper · Gherkins	**Handful 1 (+2):** · Mixed salad · Carrot · Mangetout · Gherkins	**Handful 1 (+2):** · Onion · Spring onions · Spinach
	Handful 3: · 80g ricotta cheese · 1 egg	**Handful 3:** · 120g roast beef	**Handful 3:** · 2 bacon rashers · 1 egg · 125g ricotta cheese
	Handful 4: · 30g oats	**Handful 4:** · 1 small tortilla (40–50g)	**Handful 4:** · 1 small tortilla (40–50g)
	Fat: · 5g pine nuts · 10g pecan nuts · 10g dark chocolate	**Fat:** · 20g mayonnaise	**Fat:** · ½ teaspoon olive oil · 20g cheese, min. 18% fat
OPTIONAL	**Dairy product:** -	**Dairy product:** -	**Dairy product:** · 25ml skimmed milk
	Dairy dressing: -	**Dairy dressing:** -	**Dairy dressing:** -
UNRESTRICTED IN SMALL QUANTITIES	**Flavourings:** · Salt · Pepper · Cress · Honey · Sorrel	**Flavourings:** · Mango chutney · Curry powder · Salt · Pepper · Wild garlic	**Flavourings:** · Garlic · Nutmeg · Salt · Pepper · Pea shoots · Nasturtiums

Optional snack between meals: Bouillon drink

Day 6, woman – total 1775kcal

	MEAL-BOX 1: 576KCAL Pancakes	MEAL-BOX 2: 586KCAL Tuna fishcakes with rye	MEAL-BOX 3: 613KCAL Baked sweet potato with chickpeas
MOST IMPORTANT ELEMENTS IN THE DIET	**Handful 1 (+2):** · Sugar snap peas	**Handful 1 (+2):** · Sweet potato · Mixed lettuce · Spring onions · Red onion · Yellow pepper	**Handful 1 (+2):** · Sweet potato · Onion · Yellow pepper
	Handful 3: · 2 eggs · 2 egg whites	**Handful 3:** · 110g tuna · 1 egg white	**Handful 3:** · 65g chickpeas · 40g cheese, max. 17% fat
	Handful 4: · ½ banana · 15g oats · 4–6 berries	**Handful 4:** · 2 tablespoons breadcrumbs · 1 slice of rye bread	**Handful 4:** –
	Fat: · 5g almonds · 10g butter · 10g dark chocolate	**Fat:** · 1 tablespoon olive oil · 10g mayonnaise	**Fat:** · 1 tablespoon olive oil · ½ avocado
OPTIONAL	**Dairy product:** –	**Dairy product:** –	**Dairy product:** –
	Dairy dressing: –	**Dairy dressing:** · 2 tablespoons crème fraîche, max. 9% fat	**Dairy dressing:** · 2 tablespoons crème fraîche, max. 9% fat
UNRESTRICTED IN SMALL QUANTITIES	**Flavourings:** · Salt · Vanilla extract · Cinnamon or cardamom · Honey · Pansy flowers	**Flavourings:** · Garlic · Chilli flakes · Parsley · Dill · Salt · Coriander or nasturtiums	**Flavourings:** · Garlic · Chilli · Cumin · Paprika · Vegetable stock · Lemon juice · Honey · Dill · Salt · Pepper · Wild garlic

Optional snack between meals: Bouillon drink

Day 7, woman – total 1734kcal

	MEAL-BOX 1: 557KCAL **Breakfast plate with cottage cheese**	MEAL-BOX 2: 594KCAL **Caesar salad with croutons**	MEAL-BOX 3: 598KCAL **Baked salmon with lemon dressing**
MOST IMPORTANT ELEMENTS IN THE DIET	Handful 1 (+2): · Radishes · Rhubarb	Handful 1 (+2): · Lettuce	Handful 1 (+2): · Courgette · Carrot · Red pepper
	Handful 3: · 40g air-dried ham · 80g cottage cheese, max. 4.5% fat	Handful 3: · 140g roasted chicken breast · 1 anchovy fillet, if used	Handful 3: · 130g salmon
	Handful 4: · 50g watermelon · 2 pieces of crispbread	Handful 4: · 1 slice of bread	Handful 4: · 100g potatoes
	Fat: · 10g sunflower seeds · ½ avocado	Fat: · 1 egg yolk · 1 tablespoon olive oil · 20g Parmesan cheese	Fat: · 20g mayonnaise · 1 teaspoon olive oil
OPTIONAL	Dairy product: · 100ml natural yogurt	Dairy product: · 50ml natural yogurt	Dairy product: · 50ml natural yogurt
	Dairy dressing: -	Dairy dressing: -	Dairy dressing: -
UNRESTRICTED IN SMALL QUANTITIES	Flavourings: · Honey · Lemon juice · Red sorrel	Flavourings: · Garlic · Salt · White wine vinegar · Pepper · Pea sprouts or pansy flowers	Flavourings: · Salt · Garlic · Lemon juice · Pea shoots

Optional snack between meals: Bouillon drink

Day 8, woman – total 1694kcal

	MEAL-BOX 1: 528KCAL Ham on toast	MEAL-BOX 2: 564KCAL Little Gem lettuce wraps	MEAL-BOX 3: 602KCAL Homemade burger
MOST IMPORTANT ELEMENTS IN THE DIET	**Handful 1 (+2):** • Tomato • Onion	**Handful 1 (+2):** • Lettuce • Carrot • Yellow pepper • Gherkins • Peas	**Handful 1 (+2):** • Cucumber • Tomato • Red onion • Red cabbage
	Handful 3: • 80g edamame beans • 60g ham	**Handful 3:** • 3 slices of roast beef • 60g prawns • 50g diced chicken • 50g cottage cheese	**Handful 3:** • 120g minced beef • 1 bacon rasher
	Handful 4: • 1 slice of bread	**Handful 4:** • 100g watermelon	**Handful 4:** • 50–60g burger bun
	Fat: • 1 teaspoon butter • 2 slices of cheese, min. 18% fat • 1 teaspoon olive oil	**Fat:** • 30g mayonnaise	**Fat:** • 10g mayonnaise • 1 slice of cheese, min. 18% fat
OPTIONAL	**Dairy product:** –	**Dairy product:** –	**Dairy product:** –
	Dairy dressing: –	**Dairy dressing:** –	**Dairy dressing:** • 2 tablespoons crème fraîche, max. 9% fat
UNRESTRICTED IN SMALL QUANTITIES	**Flavourings:** • Mustard • Lemon juice • Salt • Pepper • Watercress	**Flavourings:** • Horseradish or garlic • Salt • Pepper • Chilli sauce • Mango chutney • Curry powder • Herbs	**Flavourings:** • White wine vinegar • Sugar • Salt • Pepper • Tomato ketchup • Paprika • Nasturtium flower

Optional snack between meals: Bouillon drink

Day 9, woman – total 1643kcal

	MEAL-BOX 1: 573KCAL Bacon and egg	MEAL-BOX 2: 525KCAL Spinach, egg and chicken wrap	MEAL-BOX 3: 545KCAL Stir-fried duck breast
MOST IMPORTANT ELEMENTS IN THE DIET	**Handful 1 (+2):** · Mushrooms · Tomato	**Handful 1 (+2):** · Spinach · Cherry tomatoes	**Handful 1 (+2):** · Oyster mushrooms · Broccoli · Spring onions · Bean sprouts
	Handful 3: · 1 bacon rasher · 1 egg · ½ can of baked beans	**Handful 3:** · 80g diced chicken · 1 egg · 1 egg white	**Handful 3:** · 140g duck breast
	Handful 4: · ½ slice of bread · 50g raspberries	**Handful 4:** · 40–50g tortilla	**Handful 4:** · 30g glass noodles
	Fat: · 1 teaspoon butter · 5g hazelnuts	**Fat:** · 30g cream cheese, min. 18% fat · 10g pine nuts · 1 tablespoon cream (38% fat)	**Fat:** · ½ tablespoon olive oil · 10g cashew nuts
OPTIONAL	**Dairy product:** · 100ml natural yogurt	**Dairy product:** -	**Dairy product:** -
	Dairy dressing: -	**Dairy dressing:** -	**Dairy dressing:** -
UNRESTRICTED IN SMALL QUANTITIES	**Flavourings:** · Salt · Pepper · Oregano · Sweet William (petals only) · Pansy flower	**Flavourings:** · Salt · Pepper · Marigolds	**Flavourings:** · Garlic · Chilli · Ginger · Teriyaki sauce · Stock · Sorrel flowers · Wild garlic
Optional snack between meals: Bouillon drink			

Recipes
for men

Recipes

ALL RECIPES SERVE 1 MAN

Breakfast

Lunch

Supper

Breakfast plate with soft-boiled egg

PREPARATION TIME: *about 30 minutes*

BASIC MUESLI:

60g rye flakes
60g spelt flakes
60g oats
2 tablespoons honey
Pinch of salt

PLUS:

1 egg
½ yellow pepper
3 slices of air-dried ham
2 slices of cheese, min. 18% fat
1 piece of crispbread
Thyme, to garnish (optional)
1 tablespoon jam or marmalade
200ml natural yogurt
30g Basic Muesli
30g berries
20g almonds

To make the Basic Muesli, toast the rye, spelt and oats in a frying pan over a medium heat. When they have browned slightly, stir the honey into the mixture and add the salt. Allow to cool and store in an airtight container.

Boil the egg for 5–6 minutes. Deseed the pepper and place the ham inside.

Place the cheese on the crispbread, garnish with thyme, and eat with a little jam or marmalade, if you like.

Pour the yogurt into a glass or bowl. Top with the Basic Muesli, berries and almonds.

WHAT YOU SHOULD HAVE ON YOUR PLATE

Half a pepper with ham. A piece of crispbread with cheese. Jam or marmelade. A glass or bowl of yogurt with Basic Muesli, berries and almonds. A soft-boiled egg.

HOW IT IS DIVIDED IN THE SCANDI SENSE MEAL-BOX

HANDFUL 1 (+ 2): *Pepper*

HANDFUL 3: *Egg, ham*

HANDFUL 4: *Muesli, crispbread, berries*

FAT: *Cheese, almonds*

DAIRY PRODUCT: *Yogurt*

FLAVOURINGS: *Honey, salt, thyme, jam or marmalade*

TIP *The Basic Muesli will keep for 2–3 weeks in an airtight container.*

TIP *You can use shop-bought muesli instead of the Basic Muesli, but make sure that the sugar content does not exceed 13g sugar per 100g of the product.*

TIP *You can use Skyr yogurt or another cultured milk product instead of natural yogurt, but make sure that the sugar content does not exceed 5g sugar per 100g of the product.*

TIP *If you are not full, there is room in the meal-box for another egg.*

Energy 731kcal · Protein 42g · Carbohydrate 57g · Dietary fibre 7.2g · Fat 36g

Cottage cheese and mango lunchbox

PREPARATION TIME: *about 10 minutes*

150g green beans, topped and tailed
1 tomato
½ red onion
½ mango
20 almonds
50g peas
1 tablespoon green pesto
200g cottage cheese, max. 4.5% fat
Salt and pepper
15g dark chocolate, min. 70% cocoa

Boil the green beans for 2–3 minutes. Drain and set aside.

Halve the cooked green beans. Cut the tomato into small pieces and finely chop the red onion. Remove the mango from its skin and cut the flesh into chunks. Roughly chop the almonds.

Combine all of the prepared ingredients in a suitable container, along with the peas.

Mix the pesto and cottage cheese together. Season with salt and pepper and serve alongside.

Serve with the dark chocolate on the side.

WHAT YOU SHOULD HAVE ON YOUR PLATE

The contents of one lunchbox and some dark chocolate.

HOW IT IS DIVIDED IN THE SCANDI SENSE MEAL-BOX

HANDFUL 1 (+2): *Green beans, tomato, red onion, peas*

HANDFUL 3: *Cottage cheese*

HANDFUL 4: *Mango*

FAT: *Pesto, almonds, dark chocolate*

FLAVOURINGS: *Salt, pepper*

TIP *If you are vegan, you can substitute the cottage cheese with pulses.*

TIP *You may prefer to use fresh vegetables, but frozen vegetables are fine.*

TIP *You can prepare this lunch the day before and safely store it overnight in the fridge.*

TIP *Instead of the almonds, you can use other nuts, grains or seeds.*

Energy 633kcal · Protein 38g · Carbohydrate 44g · Dietary fibre 13.5g · Fat 32g

Spaghetti and meatballs with courgette

PREPARATION TIME: *about 40 minutes*

TOMATO SAUCE:

2 garlic cloves
½ onion
¼ fresh chilli (optional)
1 teaspoon olive oil
½ teaspoon paprika
½ can chopped tomatoes
Salt and pepper, to taste

MEATBALLS:

200g minced pork and veal, max. 7% fat
1 tablespoon breadcrumbs
1 small egg
½ handful parsley, chopped
1 teaspoon dried oregano
½ teaspoon salt
1 teaspoon olive oil, for frying

TO GO WITH IT:

30g uncooked spaghetti
½ courgette
25g Parmesan cheese, shaved
Parsley or red basil, to garnish

Finely chop the garlic, onion and chilli, if using. Heat the olive oil in a frying pan and cook them a couple of minutes. Add the paprika and fry for a further minute before adding the tomatoes. Season with salt and pepper. Allow this mixture to simmer while you make the meatballs.

Mix all the meatball ingredients together and form small balls the size of a walnut. Fry the meatballs in olive oil for 10 minutes, shaking the pan now and then so that they brown evenly.

Cook the spaghetti, following the packet instructions.

Cut the courgette into cubes, or shred it, if you'd rather, and add to the tomato sauce 3 minutes before you are ready to serve.

Arrange everything on a dish – first the spaghetti, then the tomato sauce and courgette, and finally the meatballs. Sprinkle with Parmesan and chopped parsley or red basil.

WHAT YOU SHOULD HAVE ON YOUR PLATE

Spaghetti, tomato sauce and courgette with meatballs and Parmesan cheese.

HOW IT IS DIVIDED IN THE SCANDI SENSE MEAL-BOX

HANDFUL 1 (+2): *Onions, tomato, courgette*

HANDFUL 3: *Pork and veal, egg*

HANDFUL 4: *Breadcrumbs, spaghetti*

FAT: *Olive oil, Parmesan*

FLAVOURINGS: *Garlic, chilli, paprika, salt, pepper, parsley, oregano, red basil*

TIP *You can use only pork or only veal instead of mixed pork and veal. Or combine meat as you like.*

TIP *You can substitute extra courgette for the spaghetti if you want to avoid pasta.*

Energy 769kcal · Protein 68g · Carbohydrate 46g · Dietary fibre 11.3g · Fat 33g

Toast with ricotta, ham and tomato

PREPARATION TIME: *about 15 minutes*

RICOTTA MIXTURE:

20g pine nuts
90g ricotta cheese
Salt and pepper, to taste

TO GO WITH IT:

2 eggs
1½ slices of bread, preferably wholemeal
1 tomato
3 slices of ham
Chives, to garnish
Coffee, tea or water
50ml milk, if required

Toast the pine nuts in a dry pan over a medium heat. When they are golden brown, chop them finely and allow to cool before mixing them into the ricotta. Season with salt and pepper.

Boil the eggs for 5–6 minutes.

Toast the bread and cut the whole slice in half. Slice the tomato.

Spread the ricotta mixture on to the bread, then add the ham and tomato slices. Season with salt and pepper and garnish with chopped chives.

You can drink a cup of tea or coffee with this meal, and add milk if you want to.

WHAT YOU SHOULD HAVE ON YOUR PLATE

Three half slices of bread with topping, two soft-boiled eggs and a cup of tea or coffee.

> ### HOW IT IS DIVIDED IN THE SCANDI SENSE MEAL-BOX
>
> **HANDFUL 1 (+ 2):** *Tomato*
>
> **HANDFUL 3:** *Ricotta, egg, ham*
>
> **HANDFUL 4:** *Bread*
>
> **FAT:** *Pine nuts*
>
> **DAIRY PRODUCT:** *Milk, if used*
>
> **FLAVOURINGS:** *Salt, pepper, chives*

TIP *There is room for you to eat 15–20 almonds, a piece of dark chocolate or 10–15 olives with this meal.*

TIP *You can make do with one egg.*

Energy 686kcal · Protein 38g · Carbohydrate 41g · Dietary fibre 7.9g · Fat 40g

Chicken pasta salad

PREPARATION TIME: *about 10 minutes*

PLEASE NOTE: *The recipe uses cooked pasta.*

100g frozen edamame beans
2 tablespoons lemon juice
½ small red onion
½ red pepper
½ avocado
15g cashew nuts
25g mixed salad leaves
125g cooked chicken, diced or in strips
80g cooked pasta, preferably wholemeal

YOGURT DRESSING:

1 garlic clove
1 tablespoon chives
50ml natural yogurt
½ teaspoon salt
Sprinkling of pepper
1 tablespoon lemon juice

Place the frozen edamame beans in a bowl and pour over boiling water. Leave for a minute, then drain and toss them in a tablespoon of the lemon juice.

Finely dice the onion and pepper.

Peel and cube the avocado and toss in the remaining lemon juice.

Roughly chop the cashew nuts.

Finely chop the garlic and mix with the rest of the ingredients for the yogurt dressing.

Arrange all the items, including the chicken and pasta, on a bed of lettuce. Serve the dressing with the salad.

WHAT YOU SHOULD HAVE ON YOUR PLATE

A pasta salad with dressing.

HOW IT IS DIVIDED IN THE SCANDI SENSE MEAL-BOX

HANDFUL 1 (+ 2): *Red onion, pepper, lettuce*

HANDFUL 3: *Edamame beans, chicken*

HANDFUL 4: *Pasta*

FAT: *Avocado, cashew nuts*

DAIRY PRODUCT: *Yogurt*

FLAVOURINGS: *Lemon juice, chives, garlic, salt, pepper*

TIP *You can choose other sources of protein instead of the chicken and edamame beans – you can choose freely between other meat, fish, shellfish, low-fat cheese or pulses. You can easily use up leftovers from supper the day before.*

TIP *Instead of the pasta you can substitute rice, sweetcorn, bulgur wheat, couscous, wheat berries, even a piece of baguette – any other carbohydrate item.*

Energy 735kcal · Protein 50g · Carbohydrate 60g · Dietary fibre 12g · Fat 30g

Falafel pita with pesto dressing

PREPARATION TIME, INCLUDING BAKING TIME: *about 45 minutes*

PLEASE NOTE: *It is a good idea to let the chickpea dough rest in the fridge for 2 hours before you form into balls. However, you can make them straight away.*

FALAFELS:

140g canned chickpeas (drained weight)
1 tablespoon lemon juice
½ onion
1 garlic clove
2 tablespoons parsley
½ teaspoon ground coriander
½ teaspoon salt
½ teaspoon cayenne pepper
½ teaspoon ground cumin
1 small egg
1–2 tablespoons plain flour
1 tablespoon olive oil
1 tablespoon breadcrumbs

SALAD:

40g cherry tomatoes, sliced
40g peas
30g lamb's lettuce or other salad leaves

DRESSING:

2 large tablespoons natural yogurt
    or other low-fat dairy product
1 teaspoon red or green pesto

TO GO WITH IT:

1 pita bread, preferably wholemeal
Lemon wedges

Toss the chickpeas in the lemon juice. Roughly chop the onion, garlic and parsley. Blend in a food processor with the chickpeas. Add the coriander, salt, cayenne pepper, cumin and egg and blend to a coarse consistency.

Add just enough flour, a tablespoon at a time, so the dough is firm enough to roll into walnut-sized balls.

Place the balls on a baking sheet lined with greaseproof paper and brush them with olive oil. Sprinkle with breadcrumbs and turn them carefully. Press down lightly on them before you brush them with olive oil again and sprinkle with more breadcrumbs. Bake them in the middle of an oven preheated to 200ºC, Gas Mark 6 for 30 minutes, turning halfway through.

Arrange the salad, falafels and dressing with the pita. Garnish with lemon wedges.

WHAT YOU SHOULD HAVE ON YOUR PLATE

Two handfuls of salad, one handful of falafels, one pita bread and two to three tablespoons of dressing.

HOW IT IS DIVIDED IN THE SCANDI SENSE MEAL-BOX

HANDFUL 1 (+2): *Onion, tomato, peas, salad*

HANDFUL 3: *Chickpeas, egg*

HANDFUL 4: *Flour, breadcrumbs, pita bread*

FAT: *Olive oil, pesto*

DAIRY DRESSING: *Yogurt*

FLAVOURINGS: *Lemon juice, garlic, parsley, coriander, salt, cayenne, cumin*

TIP *If you are in a hurry, it is okay to occasionally buy ready-made falafels.*

Energy 754kcal · Protein 31g · Carbohydrate 86g · Dietary fibre 19.4g · Fat 27g

TIP
Substitute a tortilla wrap or flatbread for the pita bread.

Green smoothie

PREPARATION TIME: *about 10 minutes*

100g frozen chopped spinach
150g strawberries, frozen
200ml skimmed milk
75ml whipping cream (38% fat)
½ teaspoon vanilla extract
1 teaspoon liquid sweetener
60g cheese, max. 17% fat
4 slices of smoked saddle of pork
2–3 small carrots
3–4 radishes

Place the spinach, strawberries, skimmed milk, cream, vanilla extract and sweetener in a sturdy blender. Blend everything to make a thick smoothie. It may be necessary to stop the blender a few times, stir the ingredients and blend again.

Cut the cheese into sticks or small slices. Serve the cheese, the smoked pork and the carrots alongside the smoothie.

WHAT YOU SHOULD HAVE ON YOUR PLATE

A smoothie, half a handful of cheese, radishes, sliced meat and carrots.

HOW IT IS DIVIDED IN THE SCANDI SENSE MEAL-BOX

HANDFUL 1 (+2): *Spinach, carrots, radishes*

HANDFUL 3: *Cheese, smoked pork*

HANDFUL 4: *Strawberries*

FAT: *Cream*

DAIRY PRODUCT: *Skimmed milk*

FLAVOURINGS: *Vanilla extract, sweetener*

TIP *Add a little extra milk if you want a more liquid smoothie.*

TIP *Substitute an egg or two for the cheese, if you like.*

TIP *To make a vegan smoothie, use coconut milk, soya milk, almond milk or other plant-based products instead of cow's milk and cream.*

Energy 629kcal · Protein 38g · Carbohydrate 28g · Dietary fibre 5.9g · Fat 40g

Prawn noodle salad

PREPARATION TIME: *about 15 minutes*

DRESSING:

1 tablespoon soy sauce
15g peanut butter
2 teaspoons honey
Pinch of chilli flakes
1 tablespoon lime juice

SALAD:

50g glass noodles
50g broccoli
1 small carrot
50g bean sprouts
175g prawns
1 tablespoon chopped coriander
30g toasted cashew nuts

PLUS:

Coriander, to garnish

Combine the soy sauce, peanut butter, honey, chilli flakes and lime juice with a whisk to make the dressing.

Cover the glass noodles with boiling water and allow them to stand for 10 minutes. Drain and rinse the noodles in hot water.

Divide the broccoli into small florets and cut the carrot into matchsticks.

Combine the broccoli, carrot and bean sprouts in a bowl. Toss the vegetables in the dressing.

Add the prawns and chopped coriander.

Arrange the vegetables on top of the glass noodles and sprinkle with the cashew nuts, roughly chopped. Garnish with sprigs of coriander.

WHAT YOU SHOULD HAVE ON YOUR PLATE

Two or three handfuls of noodle salad with prawns, one handful of glass noodles.

HOW IT IS DIVIDED IN THE SCANDI SENSE MEAL-BOX

HANDFUL 1 (+ 2): *Broccoli, carrot, bean sprouts*

HANDFUL 3: *Prawns*

HANDFUL 4: *Glass noodles*

FAT: *Peanut butter, cashew nuts*

FLAVOURINGS: *Soy sauce, honey, chilli flakes, lime juice, coriander*

Energy 682kcal · Protein 43g · Carbohydrate 75g · Dietary fibre 5.9g · Fat 23g

TIP
*You can use
mint or flat leaf
parsley instead
of coriander.*

TIP

You can buy a flank steak weighing 600–800g and use the left-over meat in sandwiches for a packed lunch or as a convenient source of protein in a salad or tortilla wrap.

Marinated steak with mushrooms and cream

PREPARATION TIME: *about 25 minutes*
PLEASE NOTE: *Marinate the steak for a couple of hours in the fridge, or overnight if possible.*

MARINADE AND MEAT:

1 tablespoon muscovado or soft brown sugar
2 tablespoons soy sauce
½ tablespoon chilli flakes or paprika
Sprinkling of pepper
1 tablespoon olive oil
1 flank steak (about 200g)

MUSHROOM DISH:

2 portobello mushrooms
½ leek
1 teaspoon olive oil
80ml whipping cream (38% fat)
*½ vegetable stock cube dissolved
   in 100ml boiling water*
½ tablespoon dried tarragon
Salt and pepper, to taste

TO GO WITH IT:

40g mixed salad leaves
Fresh tarragon, to garnish

DESSERT:

1 passion fruit
1 tablespoon crème fraîche, max. 9% fat
A drop of vanilla extract
*A couple of drops of liquid
   sweetener (optional)*
5g dark chocolate, min. 70% cocoa

Mix together the marinade ingredients. Place the steak and marinade in a sandwich bag, close the bag tightly and marinate in the fridge for at least 2 hours.

Slice the mushrooms and leek. Fry the mushrooms in the olive oil for 10 minutes before adding the leek. Add the cream and stock and simmer for 10–15 minutes. Season with tarragon, salt and pepper.

Fry the steak for 6–8 minutes on each side. Allow to rest until the mushroom mix is ready. Arrange slices of steak with the mushroom mix and salad.

Cut the passion fruit in half. Stir the vanilla into the crème fraîche and add sweetener, if using. Serve a spoonful of vanilla dressing with the passion fruit and grate a little chocolate on top.

WHAT YOU SHOULD HAVE ON YOUR PLATE

One handful of salad, one large handful of the mushroom mix and one handful of steak. One passion fruit with vanilla cream.

HOW IT IS DIVIDED IN THE SCANDI SENSE MEAL-BOX

HANDFUL 1 (+2): *Mushroom, leek, salad*

HANDFUL 3: *Flank steak*

HANDFUL 4: *Passion fruit*

FAT: *Olive oil, cream, dark chocolate*

DAIRY DRESSING: *Crème fraîche*

FLAVOURINGS: *Sugar, soy sauce, chilli flakes, pepper, vegetable stock, tarragon, salt, vanilla extract, sweetener, if using*

Energy 678kcal · Protein 54g · Carbohydrate 26g · Dietary fibre 6.7g · Fat 39g

Toast with salmon and avocado cream

PREPARATION TIME: *about 15 minutes*

AVOCADO CREAM:

½ avocado
1 large tablespoon crème fraîche,
  min. 18% fat
1 teaspoon lemon juice
Salt and pepper, to taste

DRESSING:

¼ chilli
1 tablespoon mint leaves
1 tomato
1 tablespoon lemon juice
1 teaspoon white wine vinegar
Salt, to taste

PLUS:

1½ slices of bread, preferably wholemeal
60g cucumber
120g smoked salmon
Pepper, to taste
Cress or watercress, to garnish

Mash the avocado with the crème fraîche, lemon juice, salt and pepper.

Deseed the chilli. Finely chop the chilli and mint. Cut the tomato into small cubes. Toss everything in the lemon juice and white wine vinegar. Season with salt.

Toast the bread and cut it into strips. Slice the cucumber into long strips.

Spread the avocado cream to on the toast, and place the cucumber and salmon on top. Top with the dressing and garnish with cress and pepper.

WHAT YOU SHOULD HAVE ON YOUR PLATE

Strips of bread with avocado cream, cucumber and salmon with dressing.

HOW IT IS DIVIDED IN THE SCANDI SENSE MEAL-BOX

HANDFUL 1 (+ 2): *Tomato, cucumber*

HANDFUL 3: *Smoked salmon*

HANDFUL 4: *Bread*

FAT: *Avocado, crème fraîche*

FLAVOURINGS: *Lemon juice, salt, pepper, mint, chilli, white wine vinegar, watercress*

TIP *If you are in a hurry, just slice the avocado. Arrange it with the salmon and cucumber on top, with crème fraîche instead of the dressing.*

Energy 620kcal · Protein 32g · Carbohydrate 45g · Dietary fibre 8.6g · Fat 31g

TIP
It is a good idea to use a mixture of cooked and raw vegetables in a Buddha bowl.

Buddha bowl

PREPARATION TIME: *about 15 minutes*

DRESSING:

1 tablespoon tahini
1 tablespoon olive oil
½ garlic clove, crushed
1 tablespoon lemon juice
Pinch of chilli flakes
Pinch of ground cumin

BUDDHA BOWL:

50g broccoli
½ mango
50g red cabbage
90g canned kidney beans (drained weight)
90g canned chickpeas (drained weight)
50g peas
50g black olives
30g bean sprouts
10g jalapeños
½ lemon
1 tablespoon sesame seeds

Whisk the tahini, olive oil, garlic, lemon juice, chilli flakes and cumin together to make the dressing.

Cut the broccoli and mango into bite-sized pieces. Finely chop the red cabbage.

Arrange all of the ingredients side by side in bowls.

Serve with the dressing on the side.

WHAT YOU SHOULD HAVE ON YOUR PLATE

Three to four handfuls of Buddha bowl with three tablespoons of dressing.

HOW IT IS DIVIDED IN THE SCANDI SENSE MEAL-BOX

HANDFUL 1 (+ 2): *Broccoli, red cabbage, peas, bean sprouts*

HANDFUL 3: *Kidney beans, chickpeas*

HANDFUL 4: *Mango*

FAT: *Tahini, olive oil, olives, sesame seeds*

FLAVOURINGS: *Garlic, lemon juice, chilli flakes, cumin, jalapeños*

Energy 759kcal · Protein 27g · Carbohydrate 63g · Dietary fibre 23.8g · Fat 38g

Curried chicken and rice soup

PREPARATION TIME: *about 30 minutes*

½ small onion
1 small leek
½ garlic clove
2 teaspoons curry powder
½ teaspoon ground cumin
1 tablespoon olive oil
150g chicken
300ml chicken stock
½ teaspoon dried thyme
1 small tomato
½ red pepper
½ teaspoon salt
Sprinkling of pepper
2 teaspoons cornflour dissolved
    in 50ml cold water
40g rice
30ml whipping cream (38% fat)
Flat leaf parsley, to garnish

Dice the onion and slice the leek and garlic.

Heat the curry powder and cumin in a heavy-based saucepan until fragrant.

Add the olive oil, onion, leek and garlic, and fry until the onion has softened.

Dice the chicken and add it to the pan. Brown it on all sides, then add the stock and thyme. Cover the soup and let it simmer for about 20 minutes.

Cut the tomato and pepper into cubes then add to the soup. Season with salt and pepper, and thicken the soup with the cornflour mix.

In a separate saucepan, cook the rice following the packet instructions.

Heat the soup until it is hot through and add the cream.

Spoon the rice on top. Garnish with sprigs of parsley.

WHAT YOU SHOULD HAVE ON YOUR PLATE

A portion of soup with rice, garnished with parsley.

HOW IT IS DIVIDED IN THE SCANDI SENSE MEAL-BOX

HANDFUL 1 (+ 2): *Onion, leek, tomato, red pepper*

HANDFUL 3: *Chicken*

HANDFUL 4: *Cornflour, rice*

FAT: *Olive oil, cream*

FLAVOURINGS: *Curry powder, cumin, garlic, stock, thyme, salt, pepper, parsley*

Energy 720kcal · Protein 41g · Carbohydrate 54g, Dietary fibre 7.5g · Fat 36g

TIP
Substitute chives or coriander for the parsley.

Porridge with stuffed pepper

PREPARATION TIME: *about 15 minutes*

STUFFED PEPPER:

10g pine nuts
½ red pepper
120g ricotta cheese
Salt and pepper, to taste
Cress, to garnish

PORRIDGE:

30g oats
200ml water
Pinch of salt
1 egg
15g pecan nuts
15g dark chocolate, min. 70% cocoa
1 teaspoon clear honey
Red sorrel, to garnish

PLUS:

2 gherkins or cornichons

Toast the pine nuts in a dry frying pan over a medium heat. Remove the seeds and white membrane from the pepper. Fill the pepper with ricotta and sprinkle the pine nuts on top. Season with salt and pepper and garnish with cress.

Place the oats, water and salt in a heavy-based saucepan. Bring to the boil, stirring continuously for a few minutes, until it has the right consistency. Break the egg into the porridge and stir until it is evenly distributed. Roughly chop the pecan nuts and chocolate.

Garnish the porridge with nuts, chocolate, honey and red sorrel. Serve with the stuffed pepper and gherkins on the side.

WHAT YOU SHOULD HAVE ON YOUR PLATE

Half a stuffed pepper, two gherkins and a bowl of porridge.

HOW IT IS DIVIDED IN THE SCANDI SENSE MEAL-BOX

HANDFUL 1 (+ 2): *Pepper, gherkins*

HANDFUL 3: *Ricotta, egg*

HANDFUL 4: *Oats*

FAT: *Pine nuts, pecan nuts, dark chocolate*

FLAVOURINGS: *Salt, pepper, cress, honey, red sorrel*

TIP *You can substitute the ricotta for quark or cottage cheese, if you like.*

TIP *You can substitute the pecan nuts for any other kind of nuts, grains or seeds.*

Energy 739kcal · Protein 26g · Carbohydrate 53g · Dietary fibre 7.5g · Fat 46g

Roast beef wrap

PREPARATION TIME: *about 10 minutes*

MANGO DRESSING:

20g mango chutney

30g mayonnaise

½ teaspoon curry powder

Salt and pepper, to taste

PLUS:

1 carrot

*1 large tortilla, preferably
  wholemeal, about 70g*

25g mixed salad leaves

50g mangetout

30g gherkins

150g roast beef, cut into strips

Mix the mango chutney, mayonnaise and curry powder to make the dressing. Season with salt and pepper.

Cut the carrot into matchsticks.

Lay the tortilla flat on a chopping board and spread half the dressing on it.

Place the salad leaves and vegetables loosely on top, then the rest of the dressing and the beef.

Fold in one end to form a base, and then fold in the two sides, so that the wrap forms an envelope.

WHAT YOU SHOULD HAVE ON YOUR PLATE

A wrap filled with one handful of vegetables, one handful of meat and some mango dressing.

HOW IT IS DIVIDED IN THE SCANDI SENSE MEAL-BOX

HANDFUL 1 (+2): *Salad, carrot, mangetout, gherkin*

HANDFUL 3: *Roast beef*

HANDFUL 4: *Tortilla wrap*

FAT: *Mayonnaise*

FLAVOURINGS: *Mango chutney, curry powder, salt, pepper*

TIP *Substitute rye bread for the tortilla.*

Energy 716kcal · Protein 41g · Carbohydrate 56g · Dietary fibre 8.4g · Fat 34g

Cheesy tortilla tart

PREPARATION TIME, INCLUDING BAKING TIME: *about 40 minutes*

SPINACH MIXTURE:

½ onion
1 garlic clove
3 spring onions
2 bacon rashers
100g frozen chopped spinach

CHEESE FILLING:

1 egg
125g ricotta cheese
½ teaspoon grated nutmeg
½ teaspoon salt
Sprinkling of pepper
25ml skimmed milk
½ teaspoon olive oil

PLUS:

1 large tortilla, preferably
  wholemeal, about 70g
25g cheese, min. 18% fat, grated
Lettuce, to garnish

Finely chop the onion, garlic and spring onions. Chop the bacon into small pieces and fry over a medium heat for a few minutes before adding the onion and garlic. Add the spring onions and spinach. Continue frying until the spinach has fully defrosted.

Whisk together the egg, ricotta, nutmeg, salt, pepper and milk to make a smooth custard.

Brush a suitable ovenproof dish with the olive oil and place the tortilla in the dish. Press it into the edges.

Put the filling in the tortilla in the following order: half of the spinach mixture, half of the cheese filling, the rest of the spinach mixture, the rest of the cheese filling. Top with the grated cheese.

Bake in an oven preheated to 200°C, Gas Mark 6 for 30 minutes. Garnish with lettuce and serve.

WHAT YOU SHOULD HAVE ON YOUR PLATE

A tortilla tart with a little lettuce on top.

HOW IT IS DIVIDED IN
THE SCANDI SENSE MEAL-BOX

HANDFUL 1 (+ 2): *Onion, spring onions, spinach, lettuce*

HANDFUL 3: *Bacon, egg, ricotta*

HANDFUL 4: *Wholemeal tortilla*

FAT: *Olive oil, cheese*

DAIRY PRODUCT: *Skimmed milk*

FLAVOURINGS: *Garlic, nutmeg, salt, pepper*

TIP *Season with your favourite herb, for example 1 tablespoon dried thyme instead of nutmeg.*

TIP *Why not make an extra as an easy lunch for tomorrow?*

Energy 718kcal · Protein 38g · Carbohydrate 46g · Dietary fibre 9.4g · Fat 40g

Pancakes

PREPARATION TIME, INCLUDING RESTING TIME: *about 30 minutes*

PLEASE NOTE: *This makes enough batter for 5–7 small pancakes, which constitutes 1 portion.*

PANCAKE BATTER:

¾ small banana

22g oats

3 eggs

2 egg whites

Pinch of salt

½ teaspoon vanilla extract

½ teaspoon ground cinnamon or cardamom

1 tablespoon honey

PLUS:

10g almonds

15g dark chocolate, min. 70% cocoa

15g butter

5–7 berries

TO GO WITH IT:

100g sugar snap peas

Place all the ingredients for the pancake batter in a blender. Blend until smooth, then allow to rest for 10–15 minutes.

Chop the almonds and chocolate into nibs.

Melt a little butter in a pan and drop the batter on in blobs. When they have begun to set, add a berry to the middle of each one. Turn them over when the batter has set completely to cook the other side.

Arrange the pancakes with a sprinkling of chocolate and almond nibs on top.

Serve the peas in a bowl on the side.

WHAT YOU SHOULD HAVE ON YOUR PLATE

All of the pancakes, with chocolate and almond nibs. One handful of sugar snap peas on the side.

HOW IT IS DIVIDED IN THE SCANDI SENSE MEAL-BOX

HANDFUL 1 (+2): *Sugar snap peas*

HANDFUL 3: *Egg, egg whites*

HANDFUL 4: *Banana, oats, berries*

FAT: *Almonds, butter, dark chocolate*

FLAVOURINGS: *Salt, vanilla extract, cinnamon or cardamom, honey*

Energy 799kcal · Protein 40g · Carbohydrate 67g · Dietary fibre 9.1g · Fat 40g

TIP
Use calorie-free
sweetener instead
of honey, if you
want to avoid
added sugar.

TIP
You can use salmon, cod or other types of fresh fish instead of tuna.

Tuna fishcakes with rye

PREPARATION TIME: *about 30 minutes*

TUNA FISHCAKES:

60g sweet potato, diced
1 can of tuna (about 120g when drained)
1 egg white
1 small garlic clove, crushed
Pinch of chilli flakes
1 tablespoon chopped parsley
1 tablespoon chopped dill
½ teaspoon salt
2 tablespoons breadcrumbs
1 tablespoon olive oil

SALAD:

1 spring onion, sliced
¼ red onion, diced
¼ yellow pepper, diced
25g mixed baby lettuce leaves
2 tablespoons crème fraîche, max. 9% fat

PLUS:

1½ slices of rye bread
15g mayonnaise

Boil the sweet potato in lightly salted water for about 20 minutes.

Drain and mash the sweet potato. Mix with the tuna, egg white, garlic, chilli, parsley, dill and salt. Form into patties and press them lightly into the breadcrumbs.

Heat the tablespoon of olive oil in a frying pan and fry the fishcakes.

Make a salad with the spring onion, red onion, pepper and lettuce and arrange it on a plate.

Serve the crème fraîche in a small bowl on the side.

Spread the mayonnaise on the rye bread and serve it with the tuna fishcakes and salad.

WHAT YOU SHOULD HAVE ON YOUR PLATE

One large handful of tuna fishcakes, one handful of mixed salad and two tablespoons of crème fraîche. One handful of rye bread with mayonnaise.

HOW IT IS DIVIDED IN THE SCANDI SENSE MEAL-BOX

HANDFUL 1 (+ 2): *Sweet potato, lettuce, spring onion, red onion, pepper*
HANDFUL 3: *Tuna, egg white*
HANDFUL 4: *Breadcrumbs, rye bread*
FAT: *Olive oil, mayonnaise*
DAIRY DRESSING: *Crème fraîche*
FLAVOURINGS: *Garlic, chilli flakes, parsley, dill, salt*

Energy 668kcal · Protein 40g · Carbohydrate 53g · Dietary fibre 9.9g · Fat 31g

Baked sweet potato with chickpeas

PREPARATION TIME, INCLUDING BAKING TIME: *about 1 hour 20 minutes*

1 large sweet potato

¼ onion

1 garlic clove

¼ red chilli

½ yellow pepper

1 tablespoon olive oil

½ teaspoon ground cumin

½ teaspoon paprika

90g canned chickpeas (drained weight)

½ vegetable stock cube dissolved
    in 50ml boiling water

1 tablespoon lemon juice

1 teaspoon clear honey

½ avocado

60g salad cheese, such as Feta,
    cubed, max. 17% fat

DILL DRESSING:

2 tablespoons chopped dill

2 tablespoons crème fraîche, max. 9% fat

Salt and pepper, to taste

PLUS:

Dill, to garnish

Wrap the potato in foil and bake for an hour in an oven preheated to 200ºC, Gas Mark 6.

Finely chop the onion, garlic and chilli. Dice the pepper.

Heat the olive oil in a hot frying pan and fry the cumin, paprika and chilli for 30 seconds, then add the onion, garlic and pepper. Add the chickpeas after about 3 minutes. Let them fry for a further minute, then add the stock. Allow to simmer for a few minutes and turn off the heat.

Combine the lemon juice and honey. Cut the avocado into slices and toss in the lemon and honey mix.

Stir the dill into the crème fraîche. Season with salt and pepper.

Unwrap the sweet potato and cut a slit in the top lengthways. Squeeze the potato gently to open it up. Scrape out most of the flesh and mix it with the chickpea mixture. Add the cheese and mix until well combined. Fill the potato generously with the chickpea mixture, then place it under the grill for 3–5 minutes.

Serve with the avocado and dill dressing on top. Garnish with dill.

WHAT YOU SHOULD HAVE ON YOUR PLATE

A filled sweet potato with avocado and dill dressing.

HOW IT IS DIVIDED IN THE SCANDI SENSE MEAL-BOX

HANDFUL 1 (+2): *Sweet potato, onion, pepper*

HANDFUL 3: *Chickpeas, cheese*

FAT: *Olive oil, avocado*

DAIRY DRESSING: *Crème fraîche*

FLAVOURINGS: *Garlic, chilli, cumin, paprika, vegetable stock, lemon juice, honey, dill, salt, pepper*

Energy 677kcal · Protein 19g · Carbohydrate 57g · Dietary fibre 14.6g · Fat 39g

TIP

If you substitute tofu and soya cream for the cheese and crème fraîche, you have a vegan meal.

Breakfast plate with cottage cheese

PREPARATION TIME: *about 15 minutes*

70g radishes

70g watermelon

YOGURT IN A GLASS:

100ml natural yogurt

15g sunflower seeds

1 teaspoon clear honey

CRISPBREAD WITH TOPPING:

½ avocado

1 tablespoon lemon juice

60g air-dried ham

100g cottage cheese, max. 4.5% fat

3 pieces of crispbread

Fresh thyme and black pepper, to garnish

Clean the radishes but leave the tops on.

Cut the watermelon into slices.

Pour the yogurt into a glass or bowl and top with sunflower seeds and honey.

Slice the avocado and sprinkle with the lemon juice.

Divide the ham, avocado and cottage cheese between the pieces of crispbread.

WHAT YOU SHOULD HAVE ON YOUR PLATE

Half a handful of radishes and just under half a handful of melon. A portion of yogurt with topping and a crispbread with ham, avocado and cottage cheese.

HOW IT IS DIVIDED IN THE SCANDI SENSE MEAL-BOX

HANDFUL 1 (+2): *Radishes*

HANDFUL 3: *Ham, cottage cheese*

HANDFUL 4: *Watermelon, crispbread*

FAT: *Sunflower seeds, avocado*

DAIRY PRODUCT: *Yogurt*

FLAVOURINGS: *Honey, lemon juice, thyme, black pepper*

TIP *You can use a tablespoon of raisins instead of honey.*

TIP *You can toast the sunflower seeds in a hot pan.*

Energy 703kcal · Protein 41g · Carbohydrate 47g · Dietary fibre 8.9g · Fat 37g

Caesar salad with croutons

PREPARATION TIME: *about 20 minutes*

CAESAR DRESSING:

50ml natural yogurt
1 egg yolk
½ garlic clove, crushed
½ teaspoon salt
2 tablespoons white wine vinegar
1 anchovy fillet (optional)

PLUS:

2 Little Gem lettuces
1 tablespoon olive oil
1½ slices of bread, preferably wholemeal
Pinch of salt
1 roasted chicken breast (170g), sliced
25g Parmesan cheese, shaved
Pepper, to taste

Whisk the yogurt, egg yolk, garlic, salt and white wine vinegar together to make the dressing. Mash the anchovy fillet, if using, and stir it into the dressing.

Remove and discard the outer leaves of the lettuces and rinse.

Cut one lettuce in half and brush the cut surface with a little olive oil. Fry the cut surfaces for 1–2 minutes in a hot frying pan.

Brush the bread on both sides with the remaining olive oil, season with a pinch of salt and sauté in a hot pan until crisp on both sides.

Roughly tear the leaves from the second lettuce and spread them out on a plate.

Cut the bread into cubes and scatter the croutons over the lettuce. Place the fried pieces of lettuce on top. Equally arrange the chicken, Caesar dressing and Parmesan on top and season with pepper.

WHAT YOU SHOULD HAVE ON YOUR PLATE

Three or four handfuls of fried Caesar salad with dressing and Parmesan.

HOW IT IS DIVIDED IN THE SCANDI SENSE MEAL-BOX

HANDFUL 1 (+2): *Lettuce*

HANDFUL 3: *Chicken breast, anchovy*

HANDFUL 4: *Bread*

FAT: *Egg yolk, olive oil, Parmesan*

DAIRY PRODUCT: *Yogurt*

FLAVOURINGS: *Garlic, salt, white wine vinegar, pepper*

Energy 699kcal · Protein 57g · Carbohydrate 38g · Dietary fibre 6.8g · Fat 33g

TIP
You can also buy ready-made Caesar salad dressing

TIP
Instead of the sauce, you can use 2–3 large tablespoons of ready-made hollandaise sauce.

Baked salmon with lemon dressing

PREPARATION TIME: *about 20 minutes*

BAKED SALMON:

170g salmon
Pinch of coarse salt
½ garlic clove, crushed
1 lemon, sliced

LEMON DRESSING:

30g mayonnaise
60ml natural yogurt
2 teaspoons lemon juice
Pinch of salt

TO GO WITH IT:

150g new potatoes
50g courgette
75g carrot
50g red pepper
1 teaspoon olive oil
Red basil, to garnish

Season the salmon with the salt and garlic. Place the lemon slices in the bottom of an ovenproof dish. Place the salmon on top.

Bake the salmon in an oven preheated to 200ºC, Gas Mark 6 for about 20 minutes until tender.

Boil the potatoes.

Stir the mayonnaise, yogurt, lemon juice and salt together to make a dressing.

Cut the courgette, carrot and pepper into batons. Stir-fry them in the olive oil.

Serve the salmon with the potatoes, lemon dressing and stir-fried vegetables. Garnish with red basil.

WHAT YOU SHOULD HAVE ON YOUR PLATE

One handful of salmon, one to two handfuls of vegetables, one handful of potatoes and about 100ml lemon dressing.

HOW IT IS DIVIDED IN THE SCANDI SENSE MEAL-BOX

HANDFUL 1 (+ 2): *Courgette, carrot, pepper*

HANDFUL 3: *Salmon*

HANDFUL 4: *Potato*

FAT: *Mayonnaise, olive oil*

DAIRY PRODUCT: *Yogurt*

FLAVOURINGS: *Salt, garlic, lemon juice, red basil*

Energy 779kcal · Protein 41g · Carbohydrate 37g · Dietary fibre 6.2g · Fat 51g

Ham on toast

PREPARATION TIME: *about 15 minutes*

80g frozen edamame beans
1 tomato
½ onion
80g ham
1–2 teaspoons butter
1 slice of bread, preferably wholemeal
1 teaspoon mustard
2 slices of cheese, min. 18% fat
1 egg
1 tablespoon lemon juice
1 teaspoon olive oil
Salt and pepper, to taste
A few lettuce leaves, to garnish

Soak the edamame beans in boiling water for 30 seconds and drain. Cut the tomato and onion into slices. Fry the ham, onion and edamame beans in butter in a large, non-stick pan.

Toast the bread. Spread with the mustard. Lay the onion and ham on it and place the cheese on top. Place the toast in the pan until the cheese begins to melt. Fry an egg beside the toast in a teaspoon of butter.

Place the edamame beans in a small bowl and toss them in lemon juice and olive oil. Season with salt and pepper.

Arrange the tomato slices on top of the toast. Finish with the fried egg on top. Garnish with a few lettuce leaves.

WHAT YOU SHOULD HAVE ON YOUR PLATE

Ham, cheese and tomato on toast with a fried egg on top and edamame beans on the side.

HOW IT IS DIVIDED IN THE SCANDI SENSE MEAL-BOX

HANDFUL 1 (+2): *Tomato, onion, lettuce*

HANDFUL 3: *Edamame beans, ham, egg*

HANDFUL 4: *Bread*

FAT: *Butter, cheese, olive oil*

FLAVOURINGS: *Mustard, lemon juice, salt, pepper*

Energy 672kcal · Protein 47g · Carbohydrate 33g · Dietary fibre 9.3g · Fat 38g

TIP
You can use chickpeas or lentils instead of edamame beans.

TIP
You can use up all your leftovers for this recipe. Garnish with lots of fresh herbs.

Little Gem lettuce wraps

PREPARATION TIME: *about 15 minutes*

1 Little Gem lettuce

ROAST BEEF TOPPING:

25g carrot
25g yellow pepper
25g gherkins
15g mayonnaise
1 teaspoon shredded horseradish
   or chopped garlic
Salt and pepper, to taste
4 slices of roast beef

PRAWN TOPPING:

1 teaspoon sweet chilli sauce or paprika
15g mayonnaise
Salt and pepper, to taste
70g prawns

CHICKEN TOPPING:

15g mayonnaise
1 teaspoon mango chutney or curry powder
Salt and pepper, to taste
60g cooked chicken, diced or in strips

COTTAGE CHEESE TOPPING:

60g cottage cheese, max. 4.5% fat
25g peas
Salt and pepper, to taste

PLUS:

Fresh herbs, to garnish
100g watermelon

Separate the lettuce leaves and lay them on a plate to form four small 'bowls'.

Cut the carrot, pepper and gherkin into matchsticks. Mix the mayonnaise with the horseradish or garlic and season with salt and pepper. Roll the beef slices around small piles of vegetable matchsticks, adding a little horseradish dressing before rolling. Place on to one lettuce bowl.

Add sweet chilli sauce or paprika to the mayonnaise and season with salt and pepper. Place the prawns with the dressing on to another lettuce bowl.

Mix the mayonnaise with the mango chutney and season with salt and pepper. Place the chicken with the dressing on to a lettuce bowl.

Fill the final bowl with cottage cheese and peas. Season with salt, pepper and fresh herbs. Serve the watermelon on the side.

WHAT YOU SHOULD HAVE ON YOUR PLATE

Four lettuce bowls with toppings.
Watermelon on the side.

HOW IT IS DIVIDED IN THE SCANDI SENSE MEAL-BOX

HANDFUL 1 (+2): *Lettuce, carrot, pepper, gherkin, peas*

HANDFUL 3: *Roast beef, prawns, chicken, cottage cheese*

HANDFUL 4: *Watermelon*

FAT: *Mayonnaise*

FLAVOURINGS: *Horseradish or garlic, salt, pepper, chilli sauce, mango chutney or curry powder, herbs*

Energy 716kcal · Protein 43g · Carbohydrate 31g · Dietary fibre 6.1g · Fat 46g

Homemade burger

PREPARATION TIME: *about 25 minutes*

CUCUMBER SALAD:

¼ *cucumber or 1 baby cucumber*
2 tablespoons white wine vinegar
½ *teaspoon sugar*
Salt and pepper, to taste

BURGER FILLING:

2 slices of tomato
2 slices of red onion
50g red cabbage or other type of cabbage
150g minced beef, max. 7% fat
1 bacon rasher
1 slice of cheese, min. 18% fat
1 small burger bun, about 80–90g,
   preferably wholemeal
15g mayonnaise

CREME FRAICHE DRESSING:

1 tablespoon crème fraîche, max. 9% fat
1 tablespoon tomato ketchup
½ *teaspoon paprika*

Shred the cucumber into long, thin strips and place them in a bowl of boiling water for about 10 minutes.

Slice the tomato and onion.

Shred the red cabbage very finely – use a mandoline if you have one, but take care not to cut your fingers.

Form the meat into a large, flat patty with your hands. Fry the bacon in a non-stick pan, and when it is cooked, fry the beef patty in the same pan over a high heat for a couple of minutes on each side. Drain the bacon on kitchen paper.

Place the cheese on the beef patty.

Drain the cucumber thoroughly in a sieve. Mix the white wine vinegar, sugar, salt and pepper, and toss the cucumber in the marinade.

Warm the burger bun. Mix all of the ingredients for the crème fraîche dressing.

Spread crème fraîche dressing on the bottom half of the burger bun and spread mayonnaise on the top half. Place the cabbage on the bottom half, followed by the patty, then tomato and onion slices and finally the cucumber salad and bacon rasher.

WHAT YOU SHOULD HAVE ON YOUR PLATE
A burger.

HOW IT IS DIVIDED IN THE SCANDI SENSE MEAL-BOX

HANDFUL 1 (+2): *Cucumber, tomato, red onion, red cabbage*

HANDFUL 3: *Beef, bacon*

HANDFUL 4: *Burger bun*

FAT: *Mayonnaise, cheese*

DAIRY DRESSING: *Crème fraîche*

FLAVOURINGS: *White wine vinegar, sugar, salt, pepper, tomato ketchup, paprika*

TIP *This is easy to serve at a party, as you can do everything in advance. Your guests can assemble the burgers themselves.*

TIP *Barbecue enthusiast? Add a little barbecue spice to the patty and give it a few minutes on a hot barbecue.*

Energy 764kcal · Protein 50g · Carbohydrate 60g · Dietary fibre 7.6g · Fat 33g

TIP

*Missing chips?
If you eat half a meal-
box at breakfast and
half a meal-box at lunch,
you will have room for
a couple of handfuls
of chips with your
burger!*

Bacon and egg

PREPARATION TIME: *about 15 minutes*

2 bacon rashers
200g mushrooms
1 tomato
2 eggs
1 teaspoon butter
Salt and pepper, to taste

BEANS ON TOAST:

½ can of baked beans (210g)
1 slice of bread, preferably wholemeal

YOGURT IN A GLASS:

100ml natural yogurt
5g hazelnuts
50g raspberries
Sage or other herbs, to garnish

Fry the bacon until crisp in a non-stick frying pan. Place it on kitchen paper to soak up the excess grease.

Quarter the mushrooms and fry in the same pan, until they darken. Thickly slice the tomato. Let the mushrooms rest at one side of the pan while you fry the tomato and egg in butter on the other side. Season with salt and pepper.

Heat the baked beans in a small saucepan or in the microwave. Toast the bread.

Pour the yogurt into a glass or a bowl. Cut the hazelnuts in half and sprinkle them over the yogurt with the raspberries.

WHAT YOU SHOULD HAVE ON YOUR PLATE

Two handfuls of tomato and mushroom, two bacon rashers, two fried eggs, baked beans on toast and a portion of yogurt with nuts and raspberries.

HOW IT IS DIVIDED IN THE SCANDI SENSE MEAL-BOX

HANDFUL 1 (+ 2): *Mushrooms, tomato*

HANDFUL 3: *Bacon, eggs, baked beans*

HANDFUL 4: *Bread, raspberries*

FAT: *Butter, hazelnuts*

DAIRY PRODUCT: *Yogurt*

FLAVOURINGS: *Salt, pepper, sage or other herbs*

TIP *Not keen on baked beans? Have an extra fried egg or two instead.*

TIP *Try toasting the hazelnuts to get more flavour from them. A little pinch of salt gives the taste an extra edge.*

TIP *You could add 20g olives to this meal.*

Energy 748kcal · Protein 43g · Carbohydrate 67g · Dietary fibre 23.5g · Fat29g

Spinach, egg and chicken wrap

PREPARATION TIME: *about 15 minutes*

SCRAMBLED EGG:

2 eggs
1 egg white
1 tablespoon whipping cream (38% fat)
Salt and pepper, to taste

PLUS:

1 large tortilla, about 70g,
  preferably wholemeal
40g cream cheese, min. 18% fat
25g fresh spinach
100g cherry tomatoes, halved
100g cooked chicken, cubed
15g pine nuts

Whisk the eggs, egg white and cream together. Season with salt and pepper.

Pour the egg on to a hot pan and cook, stirring a little every now and then, until it has set. Take the pan off the heat.

Spread the cream cheese on to the tortilla and scatter the spinach leaves on top.

Top with the scrambled egg, cherry tomatoes, chicken and pine nuts. You can toast the pine nuts if you like.

WHAT YOU SHOULD HAVE ON YOUR PLATE

A tortilla wrap with two tablespoons of cream cheese, one handful of vegetables, a portion of scrambled egg, half a handful of chicken and a tablespoon of pine nuts.

HOW IT IS DIVIDED IN THE SCANDI SENSE MEAL-BOX

HANDFUL 1 (+2): *Spinach, cherry tomatoes*

HANDFUL 3: *Chicken, egg, egg white*

HANDFUL 4: *Tortilla wrap*

FAT: *Cream cheese, pine nuts, cream*

FLAVOURINGS: *Salt, pepper*

Energy 738kcal · Protein 55g · Carbohydrate 40g · Dietary fibre 7.4g · Fat 38g

TIP
Add a good sprinkling of fresh herbs to the wrap, such as chives or basil.

Stir-fried duck breast

PREPARATION TIME: *about 25 minutes*

STIR-FRY:

185g duck breast, thinly sliced
1 tablespoon olive oil
100g oyster mushrooms
100g broccoli
2 spring onions
½ garlic clove, thinly sliced
¼ chilli, thinly sliced
1cm fresh root ginger, thinly sliced
50g bean sprouts
1 tablespoon teriyaki sauce
1 teaspoon chicken stock powder
100–200ml water
15g cashew nuts

TO GO WITH IT:

40g glass noodles

Brown the duck well in olive oil in a hot wok. Remove from the pan and set aside.

Cut the mushrooms, broccoli and spring onions into small pieces and brown them quickly on all sides.

Add the garlic, chilli and ginger with the bean sprouts, teriyaki sauce, stock powder and water. Return the duck to the wok and heat through thoroughly.

Toast the cashew nuts and sprinkle them over the dish.

Boil the glass noodles in lightly salted water and serve them with the stir fry.

WHAT YOU SHOULD HAVE ON YOUR PLATE

Three handfuls of stir fry and one handful of glass noodles.

HOW IT IS DIVIDED IN THE SCANDI SENSE MEAL-BOX

HANDFUL 1 (+2): *Oyster mushrooms, broccoli, spring onions, bean sprouts*

HANDFUL 3: *Duck breast*

HANDFUL 4: *Glass noodles*

FAT: *Olive oil, cashew nuts*

FLAVOURINGS: *Garlic, chilli, ginger, teriyaki sauce, stock powder*

TIP *Thicken the sauce with a little cornflour dissolved in cold water.*

TIP *You can use turkey or chicken instead of duck.*

TIP *Combine the glass noodles with the stir fry while it is still in the wok.*

Energy 722kcal · Protein 52g · Carbohydrate 58g · Dietary fibre 7.7g · Fat 30g

REMEMBER!
Twice a day, your plate should contain a combination of the most important elements in the diet: VEGETABLES, PROTEIN, STARCH/ FRUIT AND FAT.

Men's daily diet plan

For those who want to plan

Completed nine-day diet plan – see page 87.

Handful 1 (+2):

Vegetables.

The bracketed (+2) means you can choose to have two handfuls of vegetables, but one is enough.

Handful 3:

Protein from meat, fish, eggs, poultry, low-fat cheese, pulses etc.

Handful 4:

Carbohydrates/starch from bread, pasta, rice, potatoes etc. as well as fruit.

Fat:

A tablespoonful of fat weighs 10–30g, depending on how energy-packed the food item is. A tablespoonful of butter weighs about 10g, and a tablespoonful of avocado weighs about 30g.

Dairy product:

Milk and cultured milk products up to 3.5% fat and 5g sugar per 100g.

Dairy dressing:

Dairy products with up to 9% fat.

Flavourings:

Spices, seasonings, herbs and indulgences used in small amounts to add flavour to the food.

Day 1, man – total 2,133kcal

	MEAL-BOX 1: 731KCAL Breakfast plate with soft-boiled egg	MEAL-BOX 2: 633KCAL Cottage cheese and mango lunchbox	MEAL-BOX 3: 769KCAL Spaghetti and meatballs with courgette
MOST IMPORTANT ELEMENTS IN THE DIET	**Handful 1 (+2):** • Yellow pepper	**Handful 1 (+2):** • Green beans • Tomato • Red onion • Peas	**Handful 1 (+2):** • Onion • Tomato • Courgette
	Handful 3: • 1 egg • 3 slices of air-dried ham	**Handful 3:** • 200g cottage cheese, max. 4.5% fat	**Handful 3:** • 200g minced pork and veal • 1 small egg
	Handful 4: • 30g basic muesli • 1 piece of crispbread • 30g berries	**Handful 4:** • ½ mango	**Handful 4:** • 1 tablespoon breadcrumbs • 30g spaghetti
	Fat: • 2 slices of cheese, min. 18% fat • 20g almonds	**Fat:** • 1 tablespoon green pesto • 20 almonds • 15g dark chocolate	**Fat:** • 2 teaspoons olive oil • 25g Parmesan cheese
OPTIONAL	**Dairy product:** • 200ml natural yogurt	**Dairy product:** –	**Dairy product:** –
	Dairy dressing: –	**Dairy dressing:** –	**Dairy dressing:** –
UNRESTRICTED IN SMALL QUANTITIES	**Flavourings:** • Honey • Salt • Thyme • Jam or marmalade	**Flavourings:** • Salt • Pepper	**Flavourings:** • Garlic • Chilli • Paprika • Salt • Pepper • Parsley • Oregano • Red basil

Optional snack between meals: Bouillon drink

Day 2, man – total 2175kcal

	MEAL-BOX 1: 686KCAL Toast with ricotta, ham and tomato	MEAL-BOX 2: 735KCAL Chicken pasta salad	MEAL-BOX 3: 754KCAL Falafel pita with pesto dressing
MOST IMPORTANT ELEMENTS IN THE DIET	**Handful 1 (+2):** · Tomato	**Handful 1 (+2):** · Red onion · Red pepper · Mixed salad	**Handful 1 (+2):** · Onion · Tomato · Peas · Lettuce
	Handful 3: · 90g ricotta cheese · 2 eggs · 3 slices of ham	**Handful 3:** · 100g edamame beans · 125g chicken, diced or in strips	**Handful 3:** · 140g chickpeas · 1 small egg
	Handful 4: · 1½ slices of bread	**Handful 4:** · 80g cooked pasta	**Handful 4:** · 1–2 tablespoons wheat flour · 1 tablespoon breadcrumbs · 1 pita bread
	Fat: · 20g pine nuts	**Fat:** · ½ avocado · 15g cashew nuts	**Fat:** · 1 tablespoon olive oil · 1 teaspoon pesto
OPTIONAL	**Dairy product:** · 50ml milk, if required	**Dairy product:** –	**Dairy product:** –
	Dairy dressing: –	**Dairy dressing:** · 50ml natural yogurt	**Dairy dressing:** · 2 tablespoons natural yogurt
UNRESTRICTED IN SMALL QUANTITIES	**Flavourings:** · Salt · Pepper · Chives	**Flavourings:** · Lemon juice · Chives · Garlic · Salt · Pepper	**Flavourings:** · Lemon juice · Garlic · Parsley · Coriander · Salt · Cayenne pepper · Cumin
Optional snack between meals: Bouillon drink			

Day 3, man – total 1989kcal

	MEAL-BOX 1: 629KCAL Green smoothie	MEAL-BOX 2: 682KCAL Prawn noodle salad	MEAL-BOX 3: 678KCAL Marinated steak with mushrooms and cream
MOST IMPORTANT ELEMENTS IN THE DIET	**Handful 1 (+2):** · Spinach · Carrots · Radishes	**Handful 1 (+2):** · Broccoli · Carrots · Bean sprouts	**Handful 1 (+2):** · Mushrooms · Leeks · Mixed salad
	Handful 3: · 60g cheese, max. 17% fat · 4 slices of smoked saddle of pork	**Handful 3:** · 175g prawns	**Handful 3:** · 200g flank steak
	Handful 4: · 150g strawberries	**Handful 4:** · 50g glass noodles	**Handful 4:** · 1 passion fruit
	Fat: · 75ml cream (38% fat)	**Fat:** · 15g peanut butter · 30g cashew nuts	**Fat:** · 1 tablespoon olive oil · 80ml cream (38% fat) · 5g dark chocolate
OPTIONAL	**Dairy product:** · 200ml skimmed milk	**Dairy product:** -	**Dairy product:** -
	Dairy dressing: -	**Dairy dressing:** -	**Dairy dressing:** · 1 tablespoon crème fraîche, max. 9% fat
UNRESTRICTED IN SMALL QUANTITIES	**Flavourings:** · Vanilla extract · Sweeteners	**Flavourings:** · Soy sauce · Honey · Chilli flakes · Lime juice · Coriander	**Flavourings:** · Muscovado sugar · Soy sauce · Chilli flakes or paprika · Pepper · Vegetable stock · Tarragon · Salt · Vanilla extract · Sweetener
	Optional snack between meals: Bouillon drink		

Day 4, man − total 2099kcal

	MEAL-BOX 1: 620KCAL Toast with salmon and avocado cream	MEAL-BOX 2: 759KCAL Buddha bowl	MEAL-BOX 3: 720KCAL Curried chicken and rice soup
MOST IMPORTANT ELEMENTS IN THE DIET	**Handful 1 (+2):** • Tomato • Cucumber	**Handful 1 (+2):** • Broccoli • Red cabbage • Peas • Bean sprouts	**Handful 1 (+2):** • Onion • Leek • Tomato • Red pepper
	Handful 3: • 120g smoked salmon	**Handful 3:** • 150ml kidney beans • 150ml chickpeas	**Handful 3:** • 150g chicken
	Handful 4: • 1½ slices of bread	**Handful 4:** • ½ mango	**Handful 4:** • Cornflour • 40g rice
	Fat: • ½ avocado • 1 tablespoon crème fraîche, min. 18% fat	**Fat:** • 1 tablespoon tahini • 1 tablespoon olive oil • 50g black olives • 1 tablespoon sesame seeds	**Fat:** • 1 tablespoon olive oil • 30ml cream (38% fat)
OPTIONAL	**Dairy product:** -	**Dairy product:** -	**Dairy product:** -
	Dairy dressing: -	**Dairy dressing:** -	**Dairy dressing:** -
UNRESTRICTED IN SMALL QUANTITIES	**Flavourings:** • Lemon juice • Salt • Pepper • Mint • Chilli • White wine vinegar • Cress or watercress	**Flavourings:** • Garlic • Lemon juice • Chilli flakes • Cumin • Jalapeños	**Flavourings:** • Curry powder • Cumin • Garlic • Stock • Thyme • Salt • Pepper • Parsley
Optional snack between meals: Bouillon drink			

Day 5, man – total 2,173kcal

	MEAL-BOX 1: 739KCAL Porridge with stuffed peppers	MEAL-BOX 2: 716KCAL Roast beef wrap	MEAL-BOX 3: 718KCAL Cheesy tortilla tart
MOST IMPORTANT ELEMENTS IN THE DIET	**Handful 1 (+2):** · Red pepper · Gherkins	**Handful 1 (+2):** · Mixed salad · Carrot · Mangetout · Gherkins	**Handful 1 (+2):** · Onion · Spring onions · Spinach · Lettuce
	Handful 3: · 120g ricotta · 1 egg	**Handful 3:** · 150g roast beef	**Handful 3:** · 2 bacon rashers · 1 egg · 125g ricotta cheese
	Handful 4: · 30g oats	**Handful 4:** · 1 large tortilla (70g)	**Handful 4:** · 1 large tortilla (70g)
	Fat: · 10g pine nuts · 15g pecan nuts · 15g dark chocolate	**Fat:** · 30g mayonnaise	**Fat:** · ½ teaspoon olive oil · 25g cheese, min. 18% fat
OPTIONAL	**Dairy product:** -	**Dairy product:** -	**Dairy product:** · 25ml skimmed milk
	Dairy dressing: -	**Dairy dressing:** -	**Dairy dressing:** -
UNRESTRICTED IN SMALL QUANTITIES	**Flavourings:** · Salt · Pepper · Cress · Honey · Red sorrel	**Flavourings:** · Mango chutney · Curry powder · Salt · Pepper	**Flavourings:** · Garlic · Nutmeg · Salt · Pepper

Optional snack between meals: Bouillon drink

Day 6, man − total 2,144kcal

	MEAL-BOX 1: 799KCAL Pancakes	MEAL-BOX 2: 668KCAL Tuna fishcakes with rye	MEAL-BOX 3: 677KCAL Baked sweet potato with chickpeas
MOST IMPORTANT ELEMENTS IN THE DIET	**Handful 1 (+2):** • Sugar snap peas	**Handful 1 (+2):** • Sweet potato • Mixed lettuce • Spring onion • Red onion • Yellow pepper	**Handful 1 (+2):** • Sweet potato • Onion • Yellow pepper
	Handful 3: • 3 eggs • 2 egg whites	**Handful 3:** • 110g tuna • 1 egg white	**Handful 3:** • 100ml chickpeas • 60g cheese, max. 17% fat
	Handful 4: • ¾ small banana • 22g oats • 5–7 berries	**Handful 4:** • 2 tablespoons breadcrumbs • 1½ slices of rye bread	**Handful 4:** –
	Fat: • 10g almonds • 15g butter • 15g dark chocolate	**Fat:** • 1 tablespoon olive oil • 15g mayonnaise	**Fat:** • 1 tablespoon olive oil • ½ avocado
OPTIONAL	**Dairy product:** –	**Dairy product:** –	**Dairy product:** –
	Dairy dressing: –	**Dairy dressing:** • 2 tablespoons crème fraîche, max. 9% fat	**Dairy dressing:** • 2 tablespoons crème fraîche, max. 9% fat
UNRESTRICTED IN SMALL QUANTITIES	**Flavourings:** • Salt • Vanilla extract • Cinnamon or cardamom • Honey	**Flavourings:** • Garlic • Chilli flakes • Parsley • Dill • Salt	**Flavourings:** • Garlic • Chilli • Cumin • Paprika • Vegetable stock • Lemon juice • Honey • Dill • Salt • Pepper

Optional snack between meals: Bouillon drink

Day 7, man – total 2,181kcal

	MEAL-BOX 1: 703KCAL **Breakfast plate with cottage cheese**	MEAL-BOX 2: 699KCAL **Caesar salad with croutons**	MEAL-BOX 3: 779KCAL **Baked salmon with lemon dressing**
MOST IMPORTANT ELEMENTS IN THE DIET	Handful 1 (+2): · Radishes	Handful 1 (+2): · Lettuce	Handful 1 (+2): · Courgette · Carrot · Red pepper
	Handful 3: · 60g air-dried ham · 100g cottage cheese, max. 4.5% fat	Handful 3: · 170g roasted chicken breast · 1 anchovy fillet, if used	Handful 3: · 170g salmon
	Handful 4: · 70g watermelon · 3 pieces of crispbread	Handful 4: · 1½ slices of bread	Handful 4: · 150g potatoes
	Fat: · 15g sunflower seeds · ½ avocado	Fat: · 1 egg yolk · 1 tablespoon olive oil · 25g Parmesan cheese	Fat: · 30g mayonnaise · 1 teaspoon olive oil
OPTIONAL	Dairy product: · 100ml natural yogurt	Dairy product: · 50ml natural yogurt	Dairy product: · 60ml natural yogurt
	Dairy dressing: –	Dairy dressing: –	Dairy dressing: –
UNRESTRICTED IN SMALL QUANTITIES	Flavourings: · Honey · Lemon juice · Thyme · Pepper	Flavourings: · Garlic · Salt · White wine vinegar · Pepper	Flavourings: · Salt · Garlic · Lemon juice · Red basil
Optional snack between meals: Bouillon drink			

Day 8, man – total 2152kcal

	MEAL-BOX 1: 672KCAL Ham on toast	MEAL-BOX 2: 716KCAL Little Gem lettuce wraps	MEAL-BOX 3: 764KCAL Homemade burger
MOST IMPORTANT ELEMENTS IN THE DIET	**Handful 1 (+2):** • Tomato • Onion • Lettuce	**Handful 1 (+2):** • Lettuce • Carrot • Yellow pepper • Gherkins • Peas	**Handful 1 (+2):** • Cucumber • Tomato • Red onion • Red cabbage
	Handful 3: • 80g edamame beans • 80g ham • 1 egg	**Handful 3:** • 4 slices of roast beef • 70g prawns • 60g diced chicken • 60g cottage cheese	**Handful 3:** • 150g minced beef • 1 bacon rasher
	Handful 4: • 1 slice of bread	**Handful 4:** • 100g watermelon	**Handful 4:** • 80–90g burger bun
	Fat: • 1–2 teaspoons butter • 2 slices of cheese, min. 18% fat • 1 teaspoon olive oil	**Fat:** • 45g mayonnaise	**Fat:** • 15g mayonnaise • 1 slice of cheese, min. 18% fat
OPTIONAL	**Dairy product:** –	**Dairy product:** –	**Dairy product:** –
	Dairy dressing: –	**Dairy dressing:** –	**Dairy dressing:** • 1 tablespoon crème fraîche, max. 9% fat
UNRESTRICTED IN SMALL QUANTITIES	**Flavourings:** • Mustard • Lemon juice • Salt • Pepper	**Flavourings:** • Horseradish or garlic • Salt • Pepper • Chilli sauce • Mango chutney or curry powder • Herbs	**Flavourings:** • White wine vinegar • Sugar • Salt • Pepper • Tomato ketchup • Paprika
Optional snack between meals: Bouillon drink			

Day 9, man – total 2,208kcal

	MEAL-BOX 1: 748KCAL Bacon and egg	MEAL-BOX 2: 738KCAL Spinach, egg and chicken wrap	MEAL-BOX 3: 722KCAL Stir-fried duck breast
MOST IMPORTANT ELEMENTS IN THE DIET	**Handful 1 (+2):** · Mushroom · Tomato	**Handful 1 (+2):** · Spinach · Cherry tomatoes	**Handful 1 (+2):** · Oyster mushrooms · Broccoli · Spring onions · Bean sprouts
	Handful 3: · 2 bacon rashers · 2 eggs · ½ can of baked beans	**Handful 3:** · 100g cubed chicken · 2 eggs · 1 egg white	**Handful 3:** · 185g duck breast
	Handful 4: · 1 slice of bread · 50g raspberries	**Handful 4:** · 1 large tortilla (70g)	**Handful 4:** · 40g glass noodles
	Fat: · 1 teaspoon butter · 5g hazelnuts	**Fat:** · 40g cream cheese, min. 18% fat · 15g pine nuts · 1 tablespoon cream (38% fat)	**Fat:** · 1 tablespoon olive oil · 15g cashew nuts
OPTIONAL	**Dairy product:** · 100ml natural yogurt	**Dairy product:** -	**Dairy product:** -
	Dairy dressing: -	**Dairy dressing:** -	**Dairy dressing:** -
UNRESTRICTED IN SMALL QUANTITIES	**Flavourings:** · Sage or other herbs · Salt · Pepper	**Flavourings:** · Salt · Pepper	**Flavourings:** · Garlic · Chilli · Ginger · Teriyaki sauce · Stock powder

Optional snack between meals: Bouillon drink

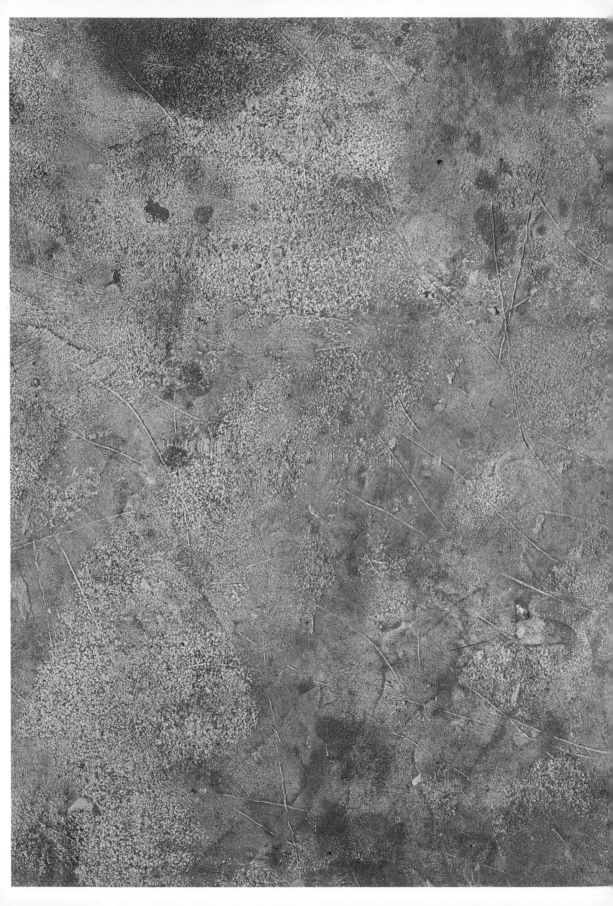

Food
directory

Handful 1 (+2): Vegetables

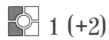 1 (+2)

Vegetables are a fantastic source of filling dietary fibre and important vitamins, minerals and antioxidants. You should prioritize coarse fibrous vegetables (marked with *) because they contain more dietary fibre than fine vegetables, such as cucumber and tomato. Raw vegetables are tasty, but be careful with quantities if you aren't used to eating them. Too many raw vegetables can cause digestive discomfort and wind whereas cooked vegetables are often slightly easier to digest. Root vegetables can easily be eaten in a weight loss programme as part of a varied diet. You can choose whether to settle for just one handful of vegetables per meal or whether to have two.

Quantity
One to two handfuls of vegetables correspond to 100–250g.

· Artichoke*
· Asparagus – green/white
· Aubergine*
· Bamboo shoots, raw
· Bean sprouts
· Beetroot*
· Broccoli*
· Brussel sprouts*
· Butternut squash
· Cabbage*
· Carrot*
· Cauliflower*
· Celeriac*
· Celery
· Chanterelle mushrooms*
· Chicory
· Chilli – all kinds
· Chinese cabbage
· Chinese radish/daikon
· Courgette
· Cucumber
· Fennel*

· Garlic*
· Green beans*
· Green peas*
· Hamburg parsley*
· Jalapeños
· Jerusalem artichoke*
· Kale*
· Kohlrabi*
· Leeks*
· Lettuce – all kinds (including iceberg and butterhead)
· Mung beans
· Mushrooms – all kinds
· Onions* – all kinds
· Parsnip*
· Peppers – all kinds
· Pointed cabbage*
· Pumpkin – all kinds of edible pumpkin
· Radishes – all kinds
· Red cabbage*

· Rhubarb*
· Romaine lettuce*
· Rocket
· Savoy cabbage*
· Salsify*
· Seaweed*
· Spinach*
· Spring onions*
· Sugar snap peas*
· Sun-dried tomato
· Sweet potato*
· Tomatoes – all kinds (including canned chopped tomatoes)
· Turnip*

* Coarse fibrous vegetables

Handful 3:
Protein

3

Proteins are important building blocks for the body, especially when losing weight, as they make you feel full and help to maintain muscle tissue so that you primarily lose fat.

MEAT FROM FOUR-LEGGED ANIMALS AND POULTRY

Varying your protein is important. Try to get different kinds into your meals over the course of the week. It is a good idea to restrict red meat to two or three times a week.

Quantity

A handful of meat is generally about 100–200g.

· Beef, pork and lamb
· Chicken, turkey and other poultry
· Deer, pheasant, rabbit, duck and similar

PROCESSED MEAT INCLUDING SAUSAGES, PATES, HAM AND SALAMI

When meat is processed, the risk of accumulating chemical substances increases, which can, for example, become carcinogenic. Processed meat products should therefore only be eaten a few times a week. Choose organic products and go for sausages with a high meat content.

Quantity

Don't eat more processed meat than can cover your palm in a thin layer. For example, 1–2 sausages, 1–2 tablespoons of pâté or 2–3 slices of ham, salami or bacon. Use your common sense. Supplement this type of meat with another form of protein, such as half a handful of fish or pulses.

· Bacon
· Black pudding
· Liver sausage
· Meatballs with a long shelf life
· Pâté – all kinds
· Processed ham – all kinds
· Salami
· Sausages – all kinds (including Cumberland)
· Terrine

FISH AND SHELLFISH

All marine animals are a healthy source of protein. Fish, especially the oily ones, are rich in important omega-3 fatty acids and vitamin D.

Quantity

A handful of fish or shellfish corresponds to 100–200g.

· Caviar and other fish eggs (including roe)
· Crab
· Lean fish such as cod, plaice and flounder
· Lobster
· Mussels
· Oily fish such as halibut, salmon, mackerel and herring
· Oysters
· Prawns
· Fishcakes

· Kippers

· Mackerel in tomato sauce

· Peppered mackerel, in water or oil

· Sardines

· Snails (not exactly shellfish, but they do have shells!)

· Tuna, in water or oil

EGGS

Eggs are a fantastic source of nutrition because they contain many of the essential nutrients we need. Egg white is pure protein! You can greatly increase your protein intake by including two egg whites and two whole eggs in a meal. Contrary to popular belief, eggs alone don't raise cholesterol so you can enjoy them with peace of mind. You could combine egg with another source of protein, for example, have an egg and a small handful of prawns for a main meal. In this way, you distribute your protein allowance across the categories.

Quantity
About 2–3 eggs count as a handful.

LOW-FAT CHEESE (MAX 17% FAT)

Use your common sense. The more fat the cheese contains, the smaller the handful you should eat. For example, very few people eat low-fat cream cheese in large quantities, but you can easily pep up a piece of chicken breast with 1–2 tablespoons of low-fat cream cheese.

Quantity
A handful of low-fat cheese corresponds to 80–100g.

· All kinds of low-fat cheese

· Brie

· Cheese spread

· Cottage cheese (1.5–4.5% fat)

· Fromage frais

· Grated cheese

· Quark

· Ricotta

· Salad cheese, such as Feta

· Smoked curd cheese (1–10% fat)

PULSES

Pulses contain vegetable protein
and are similar to vegetables in that
they also contain carbohydrate in the
form of starch. If you are a vegetarian,
you should eat a wide selection of
vegetables and pulses, preferably
supplemented by dairy products.

Vegetable proteins aren't as valuable
for the body as animal proteins, but they
are a good supplement in a varied diet.
Choose pulses that are frozen, canned
or dried. The dried versions often have
to be soaked overnight and then boiled.
Edamame beans can be bought frozen
and cooked in boiling water in a few
minutes. They are available both in
their shells and pre-shelled.

It is fine to brighten up your salad with
half a handful of pulses to increase the
protein content of your meal – on top of
a handful of meat or fish.

Quantity
A handful of pulses corresponds
to 150–250g.

· Baked beans
· Black beans
· Butter beans
· Chickpeas
· Lentils – all kinds
· Mixed beans
· Red kidney beans
· Soya beans (including edamame)
· Tofu
· White beans

PROTEIN POWDER

For most people, it is entirely
unnecessary to eat protein powder.
If you eat a varied diet according to
the principles of Scandi Sense, you
will get all the protein your body needs.
However, one of the day's three meals
could be replaced by a protein shake
or similar.

Quantity

One scoop of protein powder (typically
25–40g) corresponds to about one third
to a half of Handful 3.

Handful 4: Starch and/or fruit

4

This handful includes a range of carbohydrate foods.

Handful 4 can include both starch and fruit. You can combine the two groups by, for example, eating half a slice of bread and half a handful of fruit – use your common sense. The only person you cheat by eating more than a handful is yourself.

BREAKFAST CEREALS

Choose products with no more than 13g of sugar per 100g. You can easily create a homemade muesli with honey and dried fruit, but don't use so much that the muesli becomes very sweet.

Quantity

A handful of breakfast cereals corresponds to 35g for a woman and 50g for a man.

· Barley meal or rolled barley flakes
· Cornflakes

LOOK AT THE PRODUCT'S NUTRITIONAL INFORMATION AND GO FOR THE FOLLOWING:

FAT: *No more than 7g per 100g*
TOTAL SUGARS: *No more than 13g per 100g*
SODIUM: *No more than 0.5g per 100g*
DIETARY FIBRE: *At least 6g per 100g*

· Mixed rolled flakes (for example, three or five grain mixes)
· Oatmeal or rolled oats
· Rolled spelt flakes
· Rolled wheat flakes
· Rye meal or rolled rye flakes
· Weetabix

BREAD PRODUCTS

Bread contains large quantities of starch – and starch is sugar molecules. In other words, when you eat bread, you are also eating sugar! Always choose a wholemeal option, but be aware that even with wholemeal, you can't eat as much as you like. All bread affects blood sugar levels, no matter how coarse-grained it is.

Wholemeal products contain just as many calories as processed bread products, but the fibre in wholemeal products makes you feel fuller and helps blood sugar levels to stabilize. Look for the wholemeal logo on packaging. Wholemeal refers to whole grains, crushed grains and wholemeal flour. Wholemeal flour must contain at least 6g of dietary fibre per 100g.

Quantity

One handful corresponds to 1 slice of bread, 1 small roll, half a large roll or 2–3 slices of crispbread (because they are so thin and light).

· Baguette

· Bread rolls

· Crispbread

· Hot dog rolls

· Pastry dough (including filo)

· Pita bread

· Pizza dough

· Rolls

· Rye bread

· Sliced bread

· Tacos shells and similar products made from corn flour

· Tortilla wraps

· White loaves

Note: Stone Age bread is a Nordic bread product baked without flour but with seeds, nuts, eggs and olive oil. The bread therefore contains fewer carbohydrates than bread baked with flour. On the other hand, it contains a lot of fat and protein. A thin slice counts as two tablespoons of fat in the Scandi Sense model, because it consists primarily of fat. A slice of Stone Age bread can be delicious, but in general hold back on the quantity because it contains a lot of calories.

OTHER STARCH PRODUCTS

· Bulgur wheat

· Corn

· Couscous

· Durum wheat

· Farro, kamut and einkorn wheat

· Flour (preferably wholemeal)

· Pearl barley, pearl rye and pearl spelt

· Potatoes

· Quinoa

· Rice – all kinds, including brown, wholegrain and wild

· Whole spelt

· Whole wheat (including cracked)

· Wholemeal pasta (penne, lasagne, fusilli, spaghetti, etc.)

TIP: *The size of a handful varies from person to person, but it tends to correspond to energy requirements. For a small woman, 30g bread will easily be enough. 60g will suit a tall woman and up to 90g bread will satisfy most men.*

FLOUR SUBSTITUTES

A number of flour substitutes appear in sugar-free or gluten-free recipes, as well as low-carb diet recipes. Some of these products also have a high protein content. You are welcome to eat bread and cakes baked with these products instead of products baked with wheat flour, as long as you comply with the Sense Meal-Box Model. There is only one way forward in this, and that is to try them, and use your taste buds to find the ones that you like.

Note that there is a difference in where in the meal-box the different kinds of flour belong.

COUNTS AS HANDFUL 3

· Low-fat almond flour with a high protein content (min. 40%)

· Chickpea flour

· Coconut flour (fine), also known as coconut fibres (contains up to 61% fibre and is very absorbent)

· Pea flour

· Peanut flour

· Sesame flour, has a salty taste and a high protein content (min. 40%)

COUNTS AS HANDFUL 4

· Amaranth flour

· Oat bran

· Quinoa flour

· Tapioca flour

· Wheat bran

COUNTS AS FAT

· Almond flour

· Coconut flour (coarse) – can be ground to a fine flour

FRUIT

Fruit adds colour to your plate, as well as lots of beneficial vitamins, minerals and dietary fibre, but some fruits also contain a lot of sugar. Choose those with low- to medium-sugar content, and eat the fruit instead of drinking it in juice form, so that it doesn't lose its dietary fibre. If you are very fond of fruit juice, you can dilute it with vegetable juice.

Use the very sweet fruits to replace sweeteners. Fruits with a high-sugar content such as mangoes and bananas are good for smoothies. Mix fruit in with your salads, or liven up a cheese sandwich with fruit and vegetables. If you eat dried fruit, be aware that two dates or a small box of raisins are equivalent in energy to one apple. So choose small handfuls of dried fruit.

Quantity

A handful of fruit will be around 100–150g. Eat up to a handful per meal-box. One handful could be:

· 1 large fruit
· 1–2 small fruits such as mandarins, plums or similar
· 100g berries
· 1–2 fresh dates, figs, prunes or similar

LOW-SUGAR CONTENT

· Lemons
· Limes
· Raspberries
· Blackberries
· Gooseberries
· Cranberries

LOW- TO MEDIUM-SUGAR CONTENT

· Strawberries
· Pomelo
· Papaya
· Melon – all kinds
· Peaches
· Nectarines
· Blueberries
· Apples
· Apricots
· Grapefruit

HIGH-SUGAR CONTENT

· Plums
· Oranges
· Kiwifruit
· Pears
· Pineapple

VERY HIGH-SUGAR CONTENT

· Clementines
· Mandarins
· Cherries
· Grapes
· Pomegranates
· Mangoes
· Fresh figs
· Bananas
· Fresh dates
· Prunes
· Dried fruit such as dates, figs, raisins, cranberries, blueberries and mulberries

FRUITS ARE LISTED BY SUGAR CONTENT WITH THE LOWEST FIRST

1–3
tablespoons
of fat

Quantity

If you use concentrated fats such as butter, oil and mayonnaise, measure with a level tablespoon. When it comes to less concentrated fats such as nuts, avocado, crème fraîche or cheese, you can use a heaped tablespoon.

A tablespoon of fat varies from 10–30g, depending on how energy-packed the food item is. A tablespoon of butter weighs about 10g, and a tablespoon of avocado weighs about 30g.

BUTTER, COCONUT OIL AND MIXED OIL PRODUCTS

Ideally use organic butter, and avoid deep-frying, because trans fatty acids can form from intense heating over a long period of time. Trans fatty acids are processed fats that are incredibly bad for your body.

· Aioli
· Butter
· Cocoa butter
· Coconut oil
· Mayonnaise
· Palm kernel oil
· Spreadable butter/plant oil mixes

OILS

A diet with a lot of omega-6 (compared to omega-3) may upset the body's natural processes. So use an oil with a good fatty acid composition.

OILS WITH A GOOD FATTY ACID COMPOSITION

· Almond oil
· Arctic-D Cod Liver Oil and similar fish oils
· Avocado oil
· Extra virgin olive oil
· Flaxseed oil
· Hazelnut oil
· Rapeseed oil
· Walnut oil

OILS WITH A HIGH OMEGA-6 CONTENT

· Corn oil
· Grapeseed oil
· Peanut oil
· Sesame oil
· Soybean oil
· Sunflower oil
· Thistle/safflower oil

FAT FOR FRYING

Fat used for frying still counts as your 1–3 tablespoons per meal-box. Assess how much you use for frying and how much extra fat you then have available in your meal-box.

· Butter
· Coconut oil
· Duck fat
· Ghee (clarified butter)
· Goose fat
· Lard
· Olive oil
· Rapeseed oil

SAUCES, DRESSINGS AND DIPS

Keep in mind that shop-bought sauces and dressings often contain sugar and a lot of additives.

· Fatty dressings
· Fatty sauces, such as béarnaise, hollandaise, cream and butter sauces
· Hummus
· Pesto
· Tapenade
· Tartare sauce

FATTY SALADS

You can find an array of ready-made 'salads' comprising different vegetables, meat, fish or poultry. These salads are often high in fat (generally containing 65–90%) fat and should therefore be considered as an energy source under the fat group. They are processed with a long shelf life.

An alternative would be to use natural foods with an added drop of mayonnaise and a sprinkle of spices.

· Chicken salad
· Cucumber and radish salad
· Tuna salad
· Mackerel salad
· Prawn salad

CREAM, CREME FRAICHE AND HIGH-FAT CHEESE

The motto here is: good, in moderation! Use cream to add extra flavour to your vegetables or a tasty sauce. Use crème fraîche for soups or as a basis for a delicious dressing. Use high-fat cheese as a flavouring for salads or as topping on meat dishes.

Quantity

A tablespoon of high-fat cheese, cream or crème fraîche is about 20–25g.

· Crème fraîche (18% fat)
· Crème fraîche (38% fat)
· Cream (whipping cream and cooking cream with a fat content of 10% or more)
· Greek yogurt (10% fat)

HIGH-FAT CHEESES (18–45% FAT)

· All kinds of high-fat cheese
· Brie
· Camembert
· Cheddar
· Cheese spread
· Cream cheese
· Danish Blue
· Emmental
· Feta
· Gorgonzola
· Gouda
· Halloumi
· Mascarpone
· Mozzarella
· Parmesan
· Philadelphia
· Roquefort

NUTS AND SEEDS

Nuts and seeds contain a lot of fat. Nuts are a great food for people who want to gain weight, as you can quickly absorb a lot of energy from a small quantity. Nuts, kernels and seeds give flavour and bite to salads.

Quantity

A tablespoon of nuts weights about 15g.

· Almonds
· Blue and white poppy seeds
· Brazil nuts
· Cashew nuts
· Chia seeds
· Fennel seeds
· Flaxseeds
· Hazelnuts
· Macadamia nuts
· Nigella seeds
· Peanuts (and peanut butter)
· Pecan nuts
· Pine nuts
· Pistachio nuts
· Pumpkin seeds
· Sesame seeds
· Sunflower seeds
· Tahini
· Walnuts

FATTY FRUITS

Avocado is a fruit, but is mostly served as a vegetable because it isn't sweet. It is very nutritious and contains a lot of fat and dietary fibre. Coconuts are fun to crack and a tasty alternative to weekend sweets for children, or as a small snack. They also contain lots of dietary fibre.

Quantity

A tablespoon of fatty fruit weighs 25–40g. Three heaped tablespoons of avocado works out as about half a large avocado.

· Avocado
· Coconut milk (the high-fat version – for the light version see opposite)
· Fresh coconut
· Olives

DARK CHOCOLATE PRODUCTS

Chocolate contains a number of substances that can be beneficial to both body and soul. Go for dark chocolate with at least 70 per cent cocoa content. The higher the cocoa percentage, the less sugar there is. You can get 100 per cent chocolate, which is very bitter, but tastes good with a cup of coffee. Cocoa nibs are also bitter, but taste good mixed with muesli or as topping on a fruit salad.

You can use dark chocolate to satisfy your desire for sugar. But be careful: it should be enjoyed in small quantities.

Quantity

A tablespoon of dark chocolate generally weighs about 10g – this will be roughly one square from a large block of chocolate.

· Cocoa nibs
· Cocoa powder (baking cocoa)
· Dark chocolate

DAIRY PRODUCTS
Quantity
300ml a day.

· Buttermilk
· Semi-skimmed milk
· Skimmed milk
· Whole milk
· Fruit yogurt with a sugar content of less than 5g per 100g
· Greek yogurt, max. 2% fat
· Natural Skyr yogurt
· Skyr products with a sugar content of less than 5g per 100g

ALTERNATIVE 'DAIRY' PRODUCTS
Avoid dairy drinks with added sugar. If you would like to use alternative dairy products in your cooking or, for example, soya milk in your coffee, you will have to feel your way forward in terms of quantities. Alternative dairy products typically contain more calories than ordinary milk.

· Oat milk
· Light coconut milk
· Almond milk or other nut milks
· Rice milk
· Soya milk
· Spelt milk

DAIRY DRESSINGS
Quantity
2 tablespoons per meal-box, if you like. Choose a product with a fat content of 9 per cent or less.

SOURED DAIRY PRODUCTS SUCH AS:
· Light crème fraîche, max. 5–9% fat
· Cooking cream, max. 9% fat
· Natural yogurt, Skyr etc.

Drinks you can enjoy freely

COLD DRINKS

Be careful, don't be taken in! Many 'light' products do have a calorie and sugar content. Check the nutritional information. The product should contain only a few calories per 100ml.

· Light fizzy drinks
· Light squash
· Sparkling water
· Water

HOT DRINKS

Too much coffee and tea can cause sleep problems and hormone imbalances. However, you can buy different types of herbal teas, which can have a soothing effect and are therefore good for drinking before bedtime.

· Black tea
· Coffee (including instant)
· Herbal tea and infusions

Indulgences

If you use a little sugar or honey as part of your cooking, it is only counted as a flavouring. If you eat larger quantities from the indulgences, you have to consider how much you need to compensate for them in your meal-boxes. As little as 100g milk chocolate, cake or crisps corresponds to approximately one whole meal-box. A Big Mac or a large milkshake fill about one meal-box each.

DIFFERENT VARIETIES OF SUGAR
· Cane sugar
· Coconut sugar
· Fruit sugar/fructose
· Grape sugar
· Honey – all kinds
· Icing sugar
· Molasses
· Muscovado sugar
· Pearl/nibbed sugar
· Rock/sugary sweets
· Soft brown sugar
· Sugar for making jam
· Sweeteners with calories
· Syrup – all kinds (including agave)
· Vanilla sugar
· White sugar

SWEETS AND CAKES
· Biscuits – all kinds (including digestive biscuits)
· Boiled sweets and lollipops
· Buttercream
· Cake mixes
· Cakes – all kinds
· Chewing gum
· Chocolate bars
· Chocolate with less than 70% cocoa content
· Danish pastries
· Doughnuts
· Fruit slices and sticks
· Ice cream and ice lollies
· Lozenges
· Macaroons
· Marmalade and jam
· Marzipan
· Meringues
· Mixed sweets (including liquorice, wine gums, marshmallow, foam sweets etc.)
· Muesli bars
· Nougat
· Nut spreads
· Nutella
· Puddings such as blancmange, fromage frais and mousse
· Redcurrant jelly
· Rice cakes
· Snowballs (marshmallow snacks)
· Toffees
· Waffles

BREAKFAST PRODUCTS
· Fruit yogurts containing more than 5g sugar per 100g
· Breakfast pastries, such as croissants
· Breakfast cereals containing more than 13g sugar per 100g
· Muesli and granola products containing more than 13g sugar per 100g

FAST FOOD, TAKEAWAY AND SNACKS

· Burger meals with chips, a dip and a fizzy drink
· Candied nuts (and sweet nut mixes)
· Crisps – all kinds
· French fries
· Hot dogs
· Pizza (especially deep-pan)
· Popcorn
· Spring rolls

DRINKS WITH SUGAR

· Chocolate milk
· Coffee creamer
· Condensed and sweetened milk
· Elderflower cordial
· Energy drinks – all kinds
· Fizzy drinks
· Fruit juice – all kinds
· Fruit smoothies
· Hot chocolate
· Iced tea
· Squash

ALCOHOLIC DRINKS

If you like to have, for example, a glass of wine with a meal, you don't need to compensate for it in your meal-boxes. But use your common sense and save wine and spirits for special occasions. Bear in mind that you will lose weight more effectively if you don't drink alcohol. You can save on calories by mixing drinks with zero calorie mixers and avoiding very sweet drinks.

· Apple cider
· Beer
· Dessert wine, such as port, sherry, Asti Spumante, Madeira and Sauternes
· Drinks with syrup, fizzy drinks and juice
· Fizzy alcoholic drinks
· Sweet shots
· Spirits
· Vermouth and liqueurs
· White wine, red wine and champagne

The Danish Health Authority's recommendations on alcohol:

Women: up to 7 units per week

Men: up to 14 units per week

Flavourings

When food is flavoursome, you often feel full with smaller quantities. With Scandi Sense, you can eat as many herbs and spices as you like. This category also includes products that can be used freely, including raising and thickening agents.

HERBS AND SPICES

Herbs and spices are dried and powdered plants, or parts of a plant, that are added to food to bring out a particular taste or to add flavour. Many herbs and spices help to destroy bacteria, and some of them aid digestion. However, people who have trouble sleeping or suffer from bouts of sweating should minimize consumption of spicy food as this can aggravate restlessness and sweating. The food should taste good and be salted only as needed.

Quantity

Herbs and spices can be used freely.

· Basil
· Bay leaves
· Capers
· Cardamom
· Cayenne
· Chilli
· Chives
· Cinnamon
· Cloves
· Coriander
· Cress
· Cumin
· Curry powder
· Dill
· Garam masala
· Garlic (including garlic powder and garlic salt)
· Ginger
· Herbes de Provence
· Honey
· Horseradish
· Juniper berries
· Lemon balm
· Liquorice powder
· Marjoram
· Mint
· Mustard powder
· Nutmeg
· Oregano
· Paprika
· Parsley
· Pepper – all kinds
· Piri piri spice
· Rosemary
· Saffron
· Sage
· Salt – all kinds
· Spice mixes, such as barbecue
· Star anise
· Sugar
· Zero-calorie sweeteners
· Tandoori spices
· Tarragon

· Thyme
· Turmeric
· Vanilla extract
· Vanilla pods
· Wasabi
· Watercress

RAISING AND THICKENING AGENTS
Quantity

All raising and thickening agents can be used freely (but use your common sense). Psyllium husk and potato fibre, which are replacements for flour, can be used freely.

· Baking powder
· Cornflour (in small quantities)
· Gelatine
· Potato fibre (has a neutral taste and is very absorbent)
· Psyllium husk
· Yeast

OTHER MISCELLANEOUS FLAVOURINGS
Quantity

To be used in small quantities as needed.

· Brown sauce
· Chilli sauce
· Curry paste
· Essences and extracts
· Fish sauce
· Food colouring
· Hot sauce
· Lemon juice
· Mustard
· Sambal oelek
· Soy sauce
· Stock – all kinds
· Teriyaki sauce
· Tomato ketchup (in small quantities)
· Tomato purée
· Vinegar – all kinds (including balsamic)
· Worcestershire sauce

Scandi Sense Measurement Chart

DATE	WEIGHT	IF POSSIBLE, % FAT	R UPPERARM	L UPPERARM	CHEST	WAIST	BELLY Broadest part	

An important part of the journey towards your ideal weight is keeping and eye on your measurements and your weight. It is incredibly motivating to see how many inches and pounds disappear. Tracking the measurements will later help you to maintain your ideal weight.

L = Left   R = Right

	BACKSIDE/ HIPS Broadest part	R THIGH	R KNEE Just above the knee	R CALF	R ANKLE	L THIGH	L KNEE Just above the knee	L CALF	l ANKLE

- Choose a regular weigh-in day, once a week, so that weighing yourself becomes part of your routine. Be sure to only weigh yourself on this day and try to do it at around the same time.
- Measure yourself with a tape measure every fortnight, or as necessary.
- Always measure and weigh yourself naked.
- Make a note of the date, weight and measurements.

Index

Suzy Wengel is CEO of the Danish biotech company, RiboTask. She is a dietitian, life coach and entrepreneur married to internationally renowned scientist, Professor Jesper Wengel (who developed artificial DNA).

Suzy is 39 years old and a mother of two boys and step-mother to three children. She lost 88 pounds in 2011 using her own method – and kept it off.

An Hachette UK Company
www.hachette.co.uk

First published in Great Britain
in 2018 by Mitchell Beazley,
a division of Octopus Publishing Group Ltd
Carmelite House
50 Victoria Embankment
London EC4Y 0DZ
www.octopusbooks.co.uk

First published by as *Sense* by
J/P Politikens Hus A/S, Denmark in 2017

ISBN 978 1 78472 500 6

A CIP catalogue record for this book
is available from the British Library.

Printed and bound in Spain

10 9 8 7 6 5 4 3 2 1

Design and Illustrations: Maria Bramsen/MOM
Food Photography: Skovdal Nordic/
    Inge Skovdal
Portrait Photography: Les Kaner

For Mitchell Beazley:
Publisher: Alison Starling
Editorial Assistant: Emily Brickell
Art Director: Yasia Williams
Designer: Abi Read
Senior Production Controller: Allison Gonsalves
Translation: First Edition Translations Ltd